JAMES C. SCHAAP

THE 40-YEAR CAMPOUT

DEVOTIONS ▸ FOR

TODAY

CRC Publications

Grand Rapids, Michigan

Cover and text Illustrations: Paul Stoub

Library of Congress Cataloging-in-Publication Data
Schaap, James C., 1948-
　　　The 40-year campout / James Calvin Schaap.
　　　　　p.　cm. — (Devotions for today)
　　　ISBN 1-56212-051-4
　　　　1. Bible. O.T. Exodus XV, 22-XXXIV, 35—Devotional literature. 2. Teenagers—
Prayer-books and devotions—English. [1. Bible. O.T. Exodus—Meditations.
2. Prayer books and devotions. 3. Christian life.] I. Title. II. Title: Forty-year campout.
III. Series.
BS1245.4.S29　1993
222'.12—dc20　　　　　　　　　　　　　　　　　　　　　　93-21231
　　　　　　　　　　　　　　　　　　　　　　　　　　　　　CIP
　　　　　　　　　　　　　　　　　　　　　　　　　　　　　AC

10 9 8 7 6 5 4 3 2 1

CONTENTS

PREFACE

The second half of the book of Exodus tells the story of the developing relationship between God and the people of Israel. The Lord had demanded, "Let my people go" and forced Pharaoh to comply. And the Israelites had rejoiced in that freedom, and that they could claim this powerful God as their own.

Now as they travel though the desert of Sinai, they begin to get better acquainted with this God. They receive the laws, the rituals of worship, and the patterns of living that God demands of them. From God's perspective, this is a 40-year teaching session with a group of students that are as stubborn and rebellious as any teacher ever had.

William N. Ewer wrote:

> How odd
> Of God
> To choose
> The Jews

The sixty-four meditations in this book illustrate the truth of that little ditty. More importantly, they show that God's blessing is based not on the worthiness of those chosen but on God's own gracious choosing. As the author writes, "God doesn't say to Israel that he's blessing them as a nation because he loves the way they make sandals or cook potatoes or sing the blues. Israel didn't *earn* all this blessing—they're blessed *only* because God blessed them."

James C. Schaap, author of *The 40-Year Campout*, is a professor of English at Dordt College in Sioux Center, Iowa. His own faith and Christian perspective on life is reflected in his many short stories and articles. Besides his popular book of devotionals for teenagers, *Intermission*, Schaap has written four other books in this *Devotions for Today* series: *Someone's Singing, Lord; No Kidding, God; Take It from a Wise Guy;* and *100% Chance of Frogs.*

We offer this present book with the trust that you will enjoy it, learn from it, and gain a deeper appreciation of the teachings that we find in this part of Scripture.

Harvey A. Smit
Editor in Chief
Education Department
CRC Publications

THE GRUMBLETONIANS

....

Read Exodus 15:22-27

People grumble about a lot of things:
- *weather:* "Another drippy day—I haven't seen the sun in a year."
- *politicians:* "Those bums at city hall are fathead bozos."
- *referees:* "Hey, ump—where's your white cane?"
- *work:* "My boss is a real slave driver."
- *basketball coaches:* "That guy couldn't win with Michael Jordan."
- *moms and dads:* "They're so tight they squeak."
- *school lunch programs:* "You call that food?"

Sooner or later, we're all grumblers. When things don't go our way, most of us get a weird kind of pleasure out of slouching into our favorite corner to grumble about how bad we've got it.

Conditions have to be right for grumbling, though.

Nobody grumbles about a little brother or sister—unless, of course, that kid always gets his or her own way with Mom or Dad. And generally, nobody grumbles about food when the pantry's full. We don't grumble when we're on top.

Real world-class grumbling happens when we're flat on the bottom and perfectly powerless. We grumble about a called third strike because we know no umpire ever reverses a call. We grumble about assignments when we absolutely can't sneak out of doing them. We grumble about parents—well, because they usually call the shots.

Underdogs grumble, not honchos. Grumblers always figure they got a raw deal. They love to stew because it's all they can do.

The NIV claims the Israelites "grumbled against Moses." And who could blame them? Following God's command, Moses parts the waters of the Red Sea, accomplishing one of the great escapes of all time—only to lead the Israelites into the desert without so much as a canteen. Hey, Moses, what kind of leader are you, anyway? Really strategic planning, Moses! We haven't had a drink in three days. You call this freedom? We call it misery!

Face it, after three days without water, we'd all be thirsty too. Why put down the Jews? We'd grumble just as much as they did.

The Israelites' grumbling—murmuring, the older Bibles say—was aimed at the guy in charge, just like all grumbling is. But, as Moses knew, in this case the guy in charge wasn't Moses, but the God of heaven and earth. Unfortunately, that God takes murmuring very personally.

Grumble, grumble—murmur, murmur.

Moses catches wind of the Israelites' complaints,

and—understandably—he's angry. He doesn't grumble, though. Instead, the Bible says, he cries out to God.

God tells him to toss a tree in a swamp of ugly, brackish water. What follows is a great environmental cleanup—the water sweetens and everybody bellies up. Presto, no more grumbling.

It would be nice to say that was the end of the murmuring. One good grumble, and the Israelites cut it out forever. Nice, yes, but in fact we'll hear more grumbling in the story we're about to read, a whole lot more.

Grumble, grumble. Murmur, murmur.

Take my word for it, wandering in the desert is no picnic. What kind of freedom is this, anyway? And who exactly is this Moses? What gives him the right to boss us around? Thinks he's got a pipeline to God!

Grumble, grumble. Murmur, murmur. I'm thirsty, doggone it.

....

Dear Lord, help us to be happy. Give us the strength to be satisfied and keep us from constantly thinking about how bad we have it. Thank you for loving us, even when we aren't so lovely ourselves. In Jesus' name, Amen.

THOSE BOZO JEWS

....

Read Exodus 16:1-3

It's easy to get down on the Jews. If anybody should have had patience with Moses—and with God—they should have. After all, they witnessed all kinds of perfectly miraculous demonstrations of God's hand in their lives. How about the parting of the Red Sea, for starters?

And how about Moses tossing a tree into a swamp and turning the water mountain-fresh? And don't forget the ten plagues—to the Israelites, swarms of bugs and bloody water were hardly ancient history. Wouldn't it be great to be able to witness such miracles today?

In yesterday's reading, the Israelites, their feet still dusty from trudging across the dry Red Sea bed, started murmuring from all quarters. Tired, thirsty, dried out like beef jerky, they started questioning the whole campaign.

Moses tosses a sapling into the water, and everybody's happy.

Verse 26 of chapter 15 quotes the Lord God of Israel this way: "If you listen carefully to the voice of the Lord your God and do what is right in his eyes, if you pay attention to his commands and keep all his decrees, I will not bring on you any of the diseases I brought on the Egyptians, for I am the Lord who heals you."

Now I'll grant you, it's not so easy to trust a God who says all that when your tongue feels like sandpaper, but the Israelites had already seen more than their share of miracles. You'd think they would have said to God, "Where do I sign?"

But in today's passage they're back at it: "If only we had died by the Lord's hand in Egypt!" they grumble to Moses. "You've brought us into this mess only to kill us."

It's easy to think of the whole lot of them as two sandwiches short of a picnic. They must be crazy, turning down God's wonderful offer.

I know a doctor who sometimes wishes he treated hogs, not people. He claims that if he were a vet, he could tell a farmer to inoculate his hogs twice a day for the next forty-six months, and consider it done.

But, he says, if he tells that same farmer to quit smoking, eat broccoli, take a few pills, and not worry himself sick about getting the crops in, even money says he won't follow any of the doctor's instructions.

Even if the doctor claims that such behavior will lengthen the farmer's days, bring some spring back into his step, and make him chuckle at pain, the patient isn't likely to live up to the terms of the deal. He'll still go out back and steal a smoke after bulldozing through a full rack of barbecued ribs. Disgusting, but human.

The Lord God spells out the nature of the contract to the Israelites. "Listen," God says, "it's as simple as this: do what I tell you and you'll have the smoothest desert sailing anyone's ever seen."

But they don't. Incredible, isn't it? If you want the good life, all you have to do is follow God's instructions.

Like I said, it's easy to think of the Israelites here as foolish. But then, we share more than a few of their outstanding traits. Maybe I'm only speaking for myself here, but I'd just as soon be Daniel Boone and cut my own path as follow someone else's.

Grumble, grumble. Murmur, murmur. No thanks, Lord. It's a handsome offer, but let me do my own thing.

Stupid, maybe, but human.

Don't get it wrong. This story isn't just about the Jews.

....

Lord, thank you for your Word. No matter how interesting the stories seem, they aren't just about old times and other people. They remind us that some things don't change—that you still love your people, even when we don't deserve it. Thank you so much for your love. Amen.

THEIR DAILY BREAD

....

Read Exodus 16:4-23

God's daily gift of manna to the Israelites is one of those stories everyone knows—like Daniel in the lion's den; David and Goliath; and Samson, the hippie from Israel's muscle beach.

But manna may be a hoax. Listen to this: even today a kind of granular substance, something like frost, appears in summer on the Sinai peninsula—right where the Israelites traveled. It forms overnight under a species of tamarisk tree. Sometimes Arabs gather it in the morning, then strain it and use it like honey. They call it—believe it or not—*mann*.

Actually, *mann* isn't frost at all, but the excretion of two insects that go by the names of *Trabutina mannipara* and *Najacoccus serpentinus minor* (say that without tripping on your tongue, and win a trip to Baghdad!).

These noble insects feed on saps rich in carbohydrates and lean in nitrogen. The insects' sweet, granular excretion accumulates at night and is composed mainly of larvae and immature females (sounds great on Wheaties).

Now, if only the Israelites had had a biology teacher along, they would have known that what they were scooping up wasn't miracle food at all. In fact, they'd simply stumbled on a colony of *Trabutina mannipara* and picked up the refuse before desert ants scarfed it down.

If you believe that, I'll sell you the Sears Tower. I own it.

The great story of God's providing manna to the Israelites is really a series of miracles, not just one:

- First miracle: manna appeared regularly—not just at certain times a year, like *mann*.
- Second miracle: no matter how much they picked up, no one took home a breakfast of more than one-tenth of an ephah (that means slightly more than two quarts or 2.3 litres). Cute trick, eh? No hoarding.
- Third miracle: manna never lasted more than a day (except on the sixth day, when the Israelites were allowed to gather enough

- Third miracle: manna never lasted more than a day (except on the sixth day, when the Israelites were allowed to gather enough for the Sabbath).
- Fourth miracle: God provided the Israelites with manna for all of forty years (we're not talking about a snack attack, here, after all).

The fact is, God's highly original "fast food" wasn't *mann. Mann* appears only under the tamarisk and only at certain times of year. Manna was there for the Israelites wherever they went, no matter what the season.

In short, manna wasn't just a lucky strike. It was a miracle. After fifteen days of desert travel, the Israelites filled their empty stomachs with food. And that food nourished their souls as well. It pointed the people toward the God who was leading them.

The great thing about manna was that it was so much more than just a free breakfast. Sure, it stopped Jewish stomachs from growling. But it was also perfectly designed to stanch Israelite mouths from murmuring.

The miracle of manna points to God's favor on the Israelites. It satisfied their hunger all right, but keep in mind that ever since Adam wanted a bite of one particular fruit, we've all had ravenous appetites.

We're only on chapter 16 here; the story is far from over.

Grumble, grumble. Murmur, murmur—for forty years, and for us, thousands of years of human history. Some things don't change. Stay tuned. How'd you like to eat the same old breakfast cereal for forty years?

Manna again? Grumble, grumble. Murmur, murmur.

....

Dear Lord, you have provided for your people throughout history, and you continue to provide for us today. Thank you for the health you give us through our daily bread. Be with those this day whose health is uncertain or failing. Bring them the "manna" they need. Amen.

SABBATARIANISM

....

Read Exodus 16:24-30

Here's a basic rule about the English language: you add *ism* to a
word, and you make that word into a way of life. For instance, a *com-
mune* is a place where people work together and pool their resources.
Tack on an *ism*, and you have *communism*—a way of life that pools resources for the benefit of the whole. (Unless you've been on Saturn for
awhile, you know communism isn't too hip right now.)

Or another: an *ideal* is something that satisfies someone's idea of
what is perfect. We all should have ideals. Tack on an *ism*, and it turns
into a way of life. Charlie, here, is an idealist; he says all we have to do
is get rid of drugs and we won't have any crime. Sure.

The big word at the top of the page derives from an often-used word
in today's passage: *Sabbath*. The Sabbath, the Lord wanted the Jews
to know, was a day that simply had to be honored. Tack on an *ism*, and
the Sabbath becomes a way of life.

My father claims that when he was a boy he really disliked Sundays
because he couldn't do anything. He couldn't play ball or ride his bike
or have any fun. Just about all he could do was sit in the house and
read Sunday school papers.

When he raised his children (don't forget I'm one of them), things
changed . ... somewhat. I remember playing basketball at Skip's
house, more than a block away. It was the best driveway court around
because the basket was something less than ten feet high. I'd play for
a while with my buddies, and then go somewhere and sit because I
didn't dare go home all sweaty. Basketball was out for me, after all. On
Sunday, my dad wouldn't have approved.

Today, my son can play ball if he wants, but we still won't do some
things on Sunday. Maybe someday, like my father, my son will get
older and tell his children how incredibly strict his father (me!) was
when he was a boy. Stranger things have happened.

In today's passage God tells the Israelites to institutionalize the
Sabbath, or, to put it another way, to tack on an *ism*. All God's children
have the responsibility to set God's day apart as special. For the

Israelites, that meant gathering manna the day before the Sabbath. But just exactly how *we* should make God's day special isn't often easy to decide. Different Christians, like different generations, have different ideas.

One thing is certain: when people judge others on the basis of what they can or can't do on Sunday, we're in big trouble. God is the only judge I know of.

You see, my father thinks his dad chained him up on the Sabbath. And I think my dad was a little too uptight himself about Sunday.

But I'll give my father this much: he wanted to be obedient. My guess is, he'd say the same for his father. And I hope my son says the same for me.

The Israelites, during their long captivity in Egypt, must have simply forgotten about the Sabbath. But that miracle manna, as God explained to Moses, was meant as food for the soul as well as food for the body.

"There'll be no picking up manna on Sunday," the Lord told him. Maybe Moses thought that God was being a little too strict.

But whatever he thought, Moses knew that God wants obedience. God made it clear that the Sabbath was to be set apart. On the Sabbath, there would be no manna.

"So the people rested," the Bible says, "on the seventh day."

Obedience is still what God wants from us—obedience as a way of life.

···

*Dear Lord, sometimes it's tough to obey. Give us
the strength to do your will and to be obedient
to your word. Amen.*

THE BREAD-MAN

....

Read Exodus 16:31-36

There's a new book out by a man named Elie Wiesel, a Jewish writer who has written very often and very poignantly about World War II. Himself a victim, Wiesel spent time in the Nazi concentration camps at Auschwitz and Buchenwald, where his mother, his father, and his youngest sister all died.

Wiesel has based his career as a writer on remembering what happened, not simply because he can't forget—although that might well be true—but because he believes it is absolutely essential for people who were in the camps to tell about the horror that took place in Europe fifty years ago. He wants the world to remember the time when Hitler so mesmerized his people that they could murder millions of men, women, and children and call it *purification*.

Wiesel's new novel is titled *The Forgotten*, and the plot is incredible. A old man named Elhanan Rosenbaum, a survivor of the camps (even the youngest survivors are getting old today) begins to recognize painfully that he is becoming a victim of Alzheimer's disease.

Perhaps I don't have to tell you about Alzheimer's. Some of you may know it far better than I do. In any case, the victims of this disease lose the capacity to think—and to remember.

Most painful for Wiesel's character is his realization, as the disease begins to set in, that he will not be able to carry out the one responsibility he feels is most important—to remember and tell others about what really happened in the Nazi death camps.

A really sad plot, don't you think? It's horrible enough to look Alzheimer's disease directly in the face. But when Mr. Rosenbaum sees so painfully what lies before him—the emptiness and silence, where there needs to be spoken memories—the disease seems, if it's possible, even more tragic.

Perhaps *The Forgotten* sounds like the kind of sad book you wouldn't like to read. Wiesel would say that's precisely why you *should* read it. Who wouldn't rather go to Disney World than confront terrifying images of death camps? We'd rather not think people could do such things.

In today's passage, God clearly wants the Israelites to remember the past. God tells Moses that Aaron should pick up an omer of manna and store it away for generations to come. God wants the Israelite grandchildren to remember that when their grandparents were hungry, the Lord God Almighty gave them food, miraculously, from heaven.

But there's more to the story here. That little bit of manna, stored up forever the way it's supposed to be, points not only at the past but also toward the future. Besides reminding the Jews of God's love once long ago, the omer of manna is meant to prophesy.

You see, someday a Savior would come and become the new "bread of life." Someday this Bread-Man would deliver salvation to chronic grumblers. Someday, this Dread-Man would live up to the standards that those lowly, silly Israelites—like us—couldn't manage.

This pinch of manna is more than just a museum piece, more than just a symbol of what once was, more than just a remembrance. This pinch of manna also signifies the Word made flesh that came and lived among us murmuring people.

Wiesel is right: some things should never be forgotten.

Thank you for giving us the bread of life, Lord. Thank you for sending your Son to pay the price of our sin, for giving us life eternal. In Jesus' name, Amen.

LONG-SUFFERING

....

Read Exodus 17:1-7

I'm no math whiz, so you may want to check my calculations, but here I am on my sixth meditation and already the Israelites have been murmuring on three separate occasions. First, at the bitter water of Marah; second, when they had no food in the Desert of Sin; and again today, when they have no water at Rephidim. You've barely cracked the binding on this book, and already the refrain is all too familiar.

Grumble, grumble. Murmur, murmur.

This time their frustration is aimed in a different direction. This time, Moses says, they put the Lord God to the test (v. 2).

No longer is the Israelites' problem a simple matter of thirst. This time they murmur for some authentic proof of God. They want some demonstration, some sign of God's presence. Their testing of God takes the form of a question: "Is the Lord among us or not?"

What caused a question like that? Remember, the Israelites had reason to be sick of their journey. After all, how long can anybody walk barefoot in hot sand? Their question came straight from the heart: they were dissatisfied with their lot.

But even more, it came winging out of their disbelief. "Get the Lord to pull off some miracle for us," they grumbled. "Then at least we'll know God is out here in the middle of nowhere."

You know, that reminds me of what Christ said when some of the Pharisees asked him to put on a show of miracles, as if he were some carnival act. You know what he said? "A wicked and adulterous generation asks for a miraculous sign!" (Matt. 12:39).

As understandable as it may seem, the Israelites' request for a miracle really indicates that they didn't believe the God Moses spoke of was with them. "Hey, Moses," they say, "have God pull off something miraculous."

Now it's dangerous (not to mention impossible) to try to think like God, but just for a minute, let's play around. God's already provided these thankless grumblers with a museum of weird acts—frogs, bloody water, an angel of death, the Red Sea backed up on two sides, even daily bread simply for the gathering.

"Give us more," the people say, begging for an encore.

They've already seen enough to make it vividly clear that God is with them, for pity's sake. But, what do these blunderers beg for? Another trick, another show, another act, something wet and wild.

Now the Lord's got every right to tell them the theater is closed. No more miracles. You want tricks, hire David Copperfield or some ditzy Egyptian with a magic wand and rabbits up his sleeve.

But that doesn't happen. The real miracle of today's story is not the water from the rock. In the gallery of stunning events the Lord has pulled since Moses came on the scene, today's magic fountain rates about a two on a scale of ten.

The amazing thing is that the Lord answers the people's request at all! Once more, God stoops to the level of the murmurers and gives them a show. Once more, the Creator bends over backwards and stuns the audience. Once more, a miracle.

Long-suffering is a word we don't use much, and maybe that's okay. Who on earth is as long-suffering as the Lord? Nobody, nohow.

Hey, why don't you do a trick, Lord?

And because God loves us, God does it again! That's the miracle that stops the whole show. That's the one that brings the house down.

....

Thank you for providing for our grumbling hearts, Lord. Thank you for providing us with what we need, even when we don't deserve it. Help us spend our lives bringing thanks to your name for all that you've done for us, your people. Amen.

MEDITATION 7
THE REAL BATTLE

....
Read Exodus 17:8-16

Some people claim Vietnam changed the way people look at war because the bloody fighting of that war made its way, via television, right into North American living rooms. When you see war close up, people argue, you never glamorize it. You don't think of war as noble, even though you know people who give their lives for others in a worthy cause will always be heroes.

Maybe that's why the Pentagon kept the American press away from the deserts of Kuwait when Operation Desert Storm wrestled Saddam Hussein out of the country he'd taken over. They probably figured it this way: if nobody sees dead bodies, if they're only numbers on a sheet kicked out of a computer, then people won't have second thoughts about what is happening.

You'll notice in the passage today that the Bible tells us very little about the battle between the Israelites and Amalekites, even though it's the very first battle fought by God's people during their desert travels. There's nothing here about armor or hardware, nothing about military strategy, and no mention of the Amalekite field generals. All we really know are these basic facts: that Joshua fought against the Amalekites with some special forces, that eventually the Israelites won, and that Moses, in a weird way, determined things simply by keeping his hands in the air.

In fact, the focus of the whole report is Moses' incredible struggle to keep his hands up. For a while, it's almost funny.

I remember hearing, when I was a boy, about how tough our school's principal was. I heard he punished a kid by making him stand up in front of the class, holding a pile of books at arm's length. The principal wouldn't let him quit. Finally, the kid, who thought he was pretty tough, just wilted and fell over. I don't know if that story was true or not, but it made us all scared to death of the principal.

Now, Moses doesn't have a pile of books to keep up, but he's got the whole army of Joshua. Moses isn't fighting on the front line, but just picture him sweating bullets and trying to keep his arms up. Whenever they drop, the Amalekites beller. Aaron braces his brother's arms up again, and Joshua's boys hoot and holler.

We don't see what happens on the plain, but we know surges of strength ebb and flow according to the rhythm of Moses' tired arms. Actually, of course, the story is reported this way for a good reason The real story isn't Joshua's huge biceps, or the courage of his soldiers, or the fact that they're better spear throwers. The story of the battle is the Lord's story. That's the whole point. Not only for the Israelites, but for us. God controls the victory.

The fact is that the Israelites were only as good as the miracle (another miracle!) of Moses' arms. Was there any possible physical relationship between Moses' arms and the temper of the battle? Of course not.

God was behind the whole business. So keep your arms up, Moses. The Lord is on our side. That's why we'll win the battle. Not in our strength, but in God's. That's the real story of the war.

Not only for them either.

Not only for them, but for us.

....

All around us we see your world, Lord, and your power. Help us to rely on you in our battles, Lord. Help us to know that we can fight and win in our lives, if you are on our side. Amen.

ASTONISHED

·······························

Read Exodus 18:1-12

The New Testament parable of the rich man and Lazarus happens to be one of my favorites. Maybe it isn't as good a story as, say, the good Samaritan or the prodigal son, but I've always liked its possibilities.

Lazarus, a homeless beggar covered with boils, scoops his meals out of old Israeli dumpsters. The rich man, as you'll remember, wears Ralph Lauren rugby shirts, drives a mauve Porsche, and hasn't tasted canned food since Gerbers, back when he was a baby. He lives well.

On the other side of tomorrow, however, things change. Both men die. Lazarus rides the wings of angels into heaven. The rich man ends up greatly heated about lousy accommodations in a black lake of fire.

The rich man spots Father Abraham. "Would you send Lazarus over with some water?" he begs, "I haven't had a drink in weeks."

Abraham shakes his long silver locks. "In years past, you had your Porsche," he says. "But now it's Lazarus's turn for plush surroundings. Besides," Abraham says, "there's a moat between the two of you that no engineer can bridge."

"Then please," the rich man begs, "send Lazarus down to the home place to let my brothers know what kind of hell I'm going through."

I like the possibilities. If I were Abraham, and I had the power, I think I might have bought the rich man's idea—sent someone back from heaven or hell to tell the gospel to the rich man's fat-cat brothers. It'd be something like the ghosts who come to Scrooge in *A Christmas Carol*. Great story.

But Father Abraham shuts down the imagination. "Your brothers wouldn't believe, even if Death himself showed up at their pool," he says. "Besides, they already have Moses and the prophets."

I feel for this rich man. He figures his brothers will change their ways if only someone comes back from death to make a house call.

But Abraham says it won't make any difference. "If they don't listen to Moses and the prophets, they won't listen to Lazarus either."

Today's passage reminds me of this parable. We've been hearing a lot of grumbling from the Israelites of late, even though they've witnessed the incredible miracles of the Lord. Yet, in the passage from a couple of days ago, they claimed they still needed proof that God was real.

Now take this man, Jethro. He's been hearing outlandish stories going around the desert, stories about the Israelites' escape from the Egyptians, and he comes to bring his daughter to her husband, Moses. "Tell me the truth about these stories," he says to Moses.

So Moses tells the tales.

The NIV says Jethro "was delighted" by what he heard. Another translation says he "rejoiced" because of the stories. But the one I like claims he was *astonished*, because that word makes me think Jethro, hearing about the miracles, was not just happy, but overwhelmed.

The point is, he believed—even though he'd not seen for himself what had happened. Just hearing the stories, Jethro believed this God was for real.

Now, neither you nor I were in Egypt for all the fireworks. But God asks us to be Jethros—to believe, even though we didn't stand there and watch the whole story with our own eyes.

Pick up the Bible—right now. Go on. You've got Moses and the prophets right in your hand. What's more, you've got Jesus Christ, which is a whole lot more than Jethro or the Israelites had.

"Blessed are those who have not seen, and yet believe."

Thank you for Jethro, Lord. Thank you for showing us someone who didn't see everything firsthand, but who believed with an even stronger faith than some of the eyewitnesses did. Help us also to believe.
Amen.

DEALING WITH THE OUT-LAWS

·····································

Read Exodus 18:13-27

Mothers-in-law get all the jokes, but any married person will tell you it's smart not to cross either of the in-laws—mother or father.

In today's passage Moses does the smart thing and listens to his father-in-law, but for a more substantial reason than just keeping harmony. He listens because the advice Jethro gives makes good sense.

"You're on your way to burnout, boy," Jethro tells him. "Learn to delegate responsibility! My goodness, you aren't the only one around here with a brain."

So, the Bible says, Moses follows the advice of the first management consultant in history. He chooses some good guys from the mob of Israelites, then splits up the administration of justice.

Now don't forget that Jethro, though he provided at least one of Moses' wives, was not a Jew. He was a Midianite, and, in case you've forgotten, a priest out in the wilderness, the place where Moses hid after killing an Egyptian. He had no highly sought degrees.

In fact, Jethro was an outsider. To the Israelites he was more of an outlaw than an in-law. That's not to say he broke laws (like his son-in-law did in Egypt), he just wasn't "one of us."

Now think about this. Katy, a senior, transfers into Jefferson High when her father takes a new job in Ohio. She's always played trumpet—ever since the day she was born, she thinks. When she gets to Jefferson, she tries out for band.

The trumpet players happen to be a tight little group who've been together since junior high, and they're not terribly excited about taking in some new tooter here, somebody they don't even know.

"You know, we ought to play taps at ball games—when it's clear our team is going to win," Katy says. "We always did that at River Oaks."

The others, the tight little group, sigh painfully, as if the idea is almost poison.

"I'm just trying to help," Katy says. But the tight little group, as if on cue, stick in their mutes and start to practice.

It's not easy being an outsider—it never is.

Jethro may be Moses' father-in-law, but he's not Jewish, so Moses really doesn't have to listen to him. In spite of his public admission that the God who delivered Moses' people from the hands of the Egyptians was—surely—the only God, Jethro's an outsider.

The moral of this story is not that we all ought to listen to the new kid on the block. Outsiders can be just as wrong about things as insiders.

What's most interesting, I think, is the way God uses Jethro to accomplish some things that undoubtedly needed to be done. Moses *did* need some time off. Jethro was right, even though he wasn't a member of the "in" group.

The real story is how God uses all of us, not just those who might think themselves specially appointed, or those baptized in a specific church. Moses was a big man in the desert camp. But his God, and our God, is so very much bigger.

Sometimes it's a hard lesson for insiders like me to learn. Most often, it's not God who puts up the fences that separate us.

Dear Lord, help us not to build fences where you don't intend them. Help us to be gracious to others, even when we don't know them well. We know that you love far more of your people than we do. Help us to accept others. In Jesus' name, Amen.

MAKING A DIFFERENCE, REALLY

....

Read Exodus 19:1-6

In Phoenix, Arizona, where I used to live, a local TV station once used a verse from the Psalms every time it identified itself: "You're listening to KBOB-TV—the station that's making a difference." And then: "Blessed is the nation whose God is the Lord."

I suppose just about every Christian living in what Arizonians call "The Valley of the Sun" found their believing hearts warmed by listening to a TV station quote a Bible verse. You don't see much of the Bible on prime-time TV, except, of course, for that annual Easter extravaganza—*The Ten Commandments,* with Charlton Heston.

My guess is, someone with clout at that Phoenix station back then was a Christian. I suppose he or she thought using that little verse on the logo might help people to remember that good old America is a Christian nation.

The idea of the United States being a Christian nation goes way back to the Puritans, who thought of themselves—no kidding!—as a seventeenth-century update of God's own chosen people. They were, after all, driven out of England for their religious views. They settled a wilderness. And they fought off what they considered to be legions of heathen tribes like the Amalekites. They couldn't help but see themselves, I suppose, as a chosen people.

But before we get too pleased with ourselves, thinking we're a Christian nation, we should take a look at God's blessing to the Israelites in today's passage: "You will be for me a kingdom of priests and a holy nation."

First, the blessing doesn't imply that God is throwing in the towel on the rest of creation. Moses isn't told that by choosing the Israelites, God spurns Namibia or the Netherlands. God's chosen people aren't meant to sit around slapping each other's backs, telling each other what kind of righteous folks they really are.

As priests, the Israelites were specially chosen to minister to all of God's creation. In fact, setting the Israelites apart as God's special people wasn't intended so much for their own good, as for the good of all creation. In verse 5 God says, "The whole earth is mine."

So Israel's got no bragging rights here. Instead, there was work to be done. Israel's task was to be a whole nation of God's ministers, not a hill of couch potatoes.

And second, God doesn't bless Israel as a nation because of the way they make sandals or cook potatoes or sing the blues. Israel doesn't *earn* God's blessing—and neither can we.

The U.S. is not a Christian nation because it's got tons of megachurches or because Jerry Falwell lives here. In fact, it's not a Christian nation at all. Some Christians live in North America, and when those Christians bring the Word to society—in politics, in the arts, in their marriages, in the everyday world—then Christians here and everywhere are doing, it seems to me, what God's holy priesthood is called to do. To make a difference, really, in God's world.

> *Lord, help us not to get a big head about being your people. Give us the strength and courage to do what you would have us do—to bring the good news to your world in all kinds of ways. Amen.*

BASEBALL, APPLE PIE, AND LEVIS

....

Read Exodus 19:7-19

I'm bound to make enemies when I say this, but it seems to me that apple pie, as a symbol of American culture, is pretty silly. How many folks do you know who still spend their afternoons crimping crusts?

Baseball is legit. More people here play the game regularly—and competitively—I believe, than any other sport. (Only in frigid Minnesota does the ice stay hard enough for hockey.)

But I nominate yet another commodity to take the place of apple pie—good old jeans. Originally designed for hard work, jeans (you can call them Levis or overalls too, I guess) have become so popular that most of us—young or old, male or female—have two or three pair hanging from closet hooks.

I was a kid when, in the late sixties, jeans became really, really popular. I remember arguing that wearing jeans to church was no deep sin. My parents gave in, but only if the jeans weren't the other kind of "holey."

And today, my daughter wears shorts to church. I'm not wild about it, but when I try to argue with her, I remember too well being on her side of the argument. Memories can take the wind out of your sails.

Today, for the most part, people wear anything to church—within reason. I've seen backless dresses and cut-off shorts. I haven't seen any swimsuits yet—but then, this is Iowa.

Because there's really no such thing anymore as "Sunday clothes," it may be hard for us to understand the tough rules God lays on the Israelites concerning Mount Sinai.

"I don't want anybody touching even the foot of the mountain," God tells Moses. "They can walk up a ways *only* when they hear the ram's horn—that's it. Furthermore," God says, "everybody's got to wash their clothes, and I won't have any fooling around either—hear me?"

Moses hears all right. Just to be sure, God tells him twice.

It's easy for me to argue that this kind of warning about approaching God applies to us too. When we come to God, we shouldn't look like we've been painting gutters or pitching manure. After all, worship isn't swimming or mud volleyball.

But like I said, I remember—maybe too well—arguing for jeans. So I'm going to refrain from talking about clothes, and propose instead that God is concerned not so much with the condition of your socks or your sandals but the condition of your self.

You see, God wants our whole self—not just our soul or our mind, but *everything*. The outside of us should match what's inside. What we do with our hands should be just as holy as what's in our souls.

So far in our study of God's dealings with the newly freed Israelites, I'm struck with how important it is for us not to think of God only as some wonderful, sweetsie feeling. God is a holy being who demands our worship, our obedience, and our respect. God demanded of the Israelites—and of us—nothing less than purity, inside and out.

So, can you wear jeans to church?

Sure. Our going to church isn't the same thing as the Israelites' coming to Mount Sinai anyway. God doesn't dwell at First Church, or Riverview, or Palisades Community. God lives in us, at a million different addresses.

Nonetheless, God wants *every part* of us. Not just our emotions or our heart, but everything—body, mind and soul. Nothing less.

That "whole" kind of purity is a lot tougher than dressing up in our Sunday best, isn't it?

....

Dear Lord, help us to give you everything we have.
Help us to surrender all to your name. Fill us with
your love and power. Amen.

THE OLD TESTAMENT GOD

....

Read Exodus 19:16-25

Sometimes you hear people talk about "the Old Testament God" as if Jahweh is some different kind of being from the God of the gospels and the New Testament. And in a way, it's true. That's one reason why reading a passage like this one is so difficult for us. Moses' world was much different than ours.

Barneveld, Wisconsin, is a town not far away from a place where I once lived. In fact, when I was a high school basketball coach, my team used to play in that town. The school was a member of our conference. More often than not, we beat them.

But the gym we played in is gone now. It was razed by a massive tornado that literally blew the town away. If you go to Barneveld today, you can see that something strange happened there once, even though today, years later, the town has been rebuilt. The houses and businesses are all new, and even though Barneveld sits in the middle of the rolling, wooded hills of southern Wisconsin, the only trees in town aren't much more than saplings.

Now, if God had called the people of Barneveld, Wisconsin, before that tornado, lined them up on the downtown bank corner, and then told them to watch what was about to happen, some people might have become believers. Most likely God would have heard a chorus of wows from the assembled people.

Likewise, when the Israelites gathered at Mount Sinai and the whole place exploded, the ground trembling, thunder bellowing all over a turbulent sky, it's easy to see how the Israelites must have been roundly impressed. The Bible says they trembled. "Moses," they probably said shakily, "tell us everything God says. Don't forget a word."

Don't you wish sometimes that the Lord would still act that way—send some awesome meteorological show verifying his presence? Wouldn't you like to stand at the foot of a mountain blowing its head off, knowing that God was speaking to you? Wouldn't you like to stand in hurricane winds, knowing that God was breathing out a message?

Our God—who's also the God of the Old Testament, of course—is still the same. But no longer does God relate to us in that Old Testament way. God's name isn't written on the saw-toothed blades of lightning hurled down from heaven, or on the hurricanes called into being with a sharp snap of God's fingers. The Creator still controls nature, but no longer do we hear God say to us, as to Moses: "This is where I'll be—see to it that you watch and listen!"

And yet, today God is actually much closer to us. We live in a different era, the era that follows the coming of the Messiah. Today we have God's own Son, and when Christ left this earth to return to wherever he's seated today, he offered us the Holy Spirit.

God lives in us. Through Christ, the God with us, the Bread-Man, we're God's children. So God is all around us, not just up on Mount McKinley. God is in us, not somewhere out there.

But don't be fooled; God's nature hasn't changed. Our God is still the holy One who desires to make us, as always, believing children, holy lovers.

If you've ever huddled beneath the winds of a tornado or stood through an earthquake, you know the power of God. The Lord's hand still autographs everything around us.

God is in us now, but, believe me, God's presence is still on display if we have eyes to see.

....

We see your hand in thunderstorms, Lord, in lightning and in hail. Tornadoes witness to your power. But so do quiet summer evenings and soft breezes in April. And so do we. Help us to be witnesses of your unfailing love. Amen.

TAKE THIS PERSONALLY, PLEASE

....

Read Exodus 20:1-17

You might remember Moses standing in front of that burning bush and being told to take off his shoes. He was on holy ground, the Lord said.

That's almost the way I feel now, heading into the holy ground of the Ten Commandments. I'm in my basement, sitting in front of my Apple computer, my sandals on the floor beneath me. But I'm scared to take on those commandments. They're so important to understanding Christianity and the God we worship.

Before we start into them, one at a time, I thought it might be worth a moment to point out one little fact that's new to me—and incredibly interesting. Here it is: the commandments are directed individually.

Let me try to explain. One of the oddities of the English language is that the second person singular pronoun, *you*, is the same as the second person plural pronoun, *you*. If I said, "It's *your* turn to slop the hogs," my kids wouldn't know if I was addressing either of them or both of them. I'd have to further specify in the sentence: "It's you kids' turn to slop the hogs." Sounds horrible, but at least then they'd know I meant both of them.

So the interesting fact about the Ten Commandments, a fact English language speakers can't see because of the way the language works, is that these commandments, while being offered to the whole people of Israel, are really stated in the second personal *singular* pronoun. *You* meaning *me*.

Big deal, you say. Only an English teacher would care about that. Maybe so, but listen. Let's imagine Moses turned his delivery of the stone tablets into some kind of kids' game. Let's say that when he descended from Mount Sinai, he told God's people to take these commandments to their hearts by repeating exactly what they had to do.

"Commandment #1," he'd say. "You shall have no other gods before me."

The Israelites look at him strangely, maybe hunch their shoulders a little, and repeat: "We won't take any other gods before our God."

Moses goes into a snit. "No, no," he yells. *"You, you, you.* Not *you* as in 'all of you,' but *you* as in 'you personally.' Say it this way, '*I* won't take any other gods before *me,*'" he screams, thumbing his own chest.

The Israelites shake their heads, as if the man came down from the mountain a mite disturbed.

"Here we go again," Moses says, "*You* shall not make for yourself an idol . . ."

The people toss up their hands and stutter a little. "Ah, ah, *I* shall not make for myself an idol. . . ."

"Better," Moses yells. "Much better."

I grew up hearing the Ten Commandments read in church every Sunday morning. In that kind of public forum, I picked up the sense that this list of general moral principles are meant for all of us—and they are

But somehow, I think, they hit harder if we remember that the *you* is more specifically *me* than *us.* If we think they're *ours,* they seem kind of general, don't they? They're mine and yours.

"You (Sally, Mike, Andrea, David, Barbara, Jim, Kelly, Justin, Gerry—use your own name here) shall not misuse the name of the Lord your God."

Ouch. "I will not steal; I will not kill; I will not covet my neighbor's boat." On the stone tablets, that's the way they're written.

Dear Lord, thank you for your commandments.
They offer us a guide to living, which helps us
understand how to love our God, our neighbors,
and ourselves. Help each of us to make them ours
individually. Amen.

THE FIRST COMMANDMENT

"You shall have no other gods before me."
—Exodus 20:3

"You can always tell a hurdler by the scars on her knees."

Sandra remembered very well how Coach had told her that—four years ago already, when she'd started on the hurdles. He said she was fast enough to run sprints, but if she really wanted to win, she ought to try the hurdles. "You've got the legs for it," he said. "You're already one of the best sprinters I've got, but the way things stand, you're never going to win a state championship. You might take a few meets," he said, "but if you want the big one, Sandra—try hurdles."

So she did. And he was right. On her bedroom wall back home hung the state championship medal from last year. And this year was a cakewalk—her best time was a full second faster than anyone else in her class. She was the favorite, hands down. She could choose the college she wanted; all of them were calling. She loved the hurdles. And she was psyched up for today's race.

Sandra put her hands down, fingers spread just behind the starting line, and stretched her legs, one after the other, before setting them firmly into the blocks. What did it matter who was beside her? She ripped everything out of her mind to focus cleanly on the start—stay low, pump the arms, short steps. Fire out, hit that first hurdle full stride.

Stay low, keep your head down, spread the arms. It's a walk, she told herself. Cruise. Float like a butterfly. Piece of cake.

Sandra glanced around and that the girl next to her was praying. Oh yeah, she thought, *I'd* better get my two cents' worth in too.

"Gun's up!" the starter yelled.

Sandra checked the placement of her fingers once more, flexed her legs, turned her shoulders. Everything was loose.

"To your marks," he yelled.

The starter was a hair trigger. All morning long she'd listened to him, remembering that the time between "Set" and the shot was no more than a second. Get out of the blocks, babe, she told herself. Move that bod. Take the lead right away. Kill 'em all.

Everything in her life was aimed at this race. State champion, she thought, two years running. You want to be on the top at the awards ceremony. You want to reach down to take the congratulations of the turtles who come in second and third. You want to stand higher than anybody else. Remember last year, she told herself. What a high.

"Set."

She could burn them all, she thought. She'd given her life for this—everything. Given it all. Worked her buns off. She had it coming, she thought. Nobody works as hard as I do.

She hit the start right on the head, exploding out the very second the gun went off. Everything turned into slow motion in her head. She saw herself coming up slowly, pushing, legs churning, arms pumping.

Perfect, she thought. She was perfect.

Three strides between the hurdles. Top end. Moving, moving, moving. Everything a flow, the hurdles not even there—perfect stretch, not a thing wasted. I'm doing it, she thought. State record. State record. I want be in the books. Doggone it, she said, I want to be in the books.

I'm perfect, she thought. I'm doing it. Holy cow, I'm perfect.

So she thought. So she thought.

Lord, help us to put nothing else—not wins or successes, not money or clothes or prestige, not popularity or being part of the "in crowd"—in front of you. Bless us with peace and joy in life. In Jesus' name, Amen.

THE SECOND COMMANDMENT

....

*"You shall not make for yourself an idol in the form
of anything in heaven above or on the earth beneath
or in the waters below. You shall not bow down to
them or worship them; for I, the LORD your God,
am a jealous God, punishing the children for the sin
of the fathers to the third and fourth generation of
those who hate me, but showing love to a thousand
generations of those who love me and
keep my commandments."*
—*Exodus 20:4-6*

They say new cars nowadays don't have to be waxed, Frank told himself, but they don't know. When you do it, you know they're wrong. Something about the paint job, the way it's baked on nowadays or something. But you stand back after you wax it—you just stand there and watch the sun light it up, and you know people are stupid.

Besides, he thought, I love it. I like to stand out here and rub this stuff on like butter. You wonder if it's going to do anything at all, and then you rub it in and wait for it to dry up into, like, powder.

Man, you just gotta love it.

But if you want it do it well, you got to buy good wax. Don't get nothing on sale, nothing cute. And you got to use T-shirts—something soft cotton. Old T-shirts, ones that've been put through the wash a hundred times—soft like diapers. You need a cloth that can buff really soft, he thought. You got to stroke a car to do it right. You got to love a car.

But the real trick is buffing long enough. Most people figure once they got the wax off, the work's over. They're crazy. You want a shine—I mean, you want a wax job that's going to make your car gleam—you got to buff, baby. You got to tap the elbow grease.

Round strokes, he told himself. Round and round like a buffer. Some guys claim you can do it with a drill, a drill with a buffer. But there's nothing like a hand to really feel the car. The real thing.

Turn the cloth a lot, he told himself. He ought to write a book on it. Shoot, people would buy a book on it once they saw the way his Chevy burned. My goodness.

But you got to turn the cloth. There's a right way of doing this, he thought. Not just any moron can make a shine. You got to turn the cloth or all you do is keep streaking things.

And have enough of them. Don't skimp on the rags. There's nothing that finish likes better than a soft stroke from a clean rag. Too many people use just one rag. They figure one rag is all a car needs. Good cars need a couple of rags. You got to love your car—it's that simple.

Wear a headband, he remembered. You don't want your sweat falling on the shine. That's a crime. And you're going to sweat. You want a world-class gleam, baby, you're going to sweat. You better. You owe it to the car. Wear a headband. You don't want no salt messing the shine. No way.

Step back once in awhile. Step back and look at what you're doing because it makes going on so much easier. Look at that shine. Soak it up. It's beautiful. It's divine.

You want to attract women, you gotta wax the buggy—that's all there is to it. People say cars nowadays don't need to be waxed. They don't know how good it is to spend the time with the finish. They don't know how it feels inside. They don't know what a shine is.

And that first ride. Get in the car right away, as soon as you're done. Get in the car and tool around. You'll swear the thing runs better when it's clean. No kidding.

He knew he really ought to write a book on it.

You ought to see that buggy shine. You really ought to see that buggy shine. It's heavenly. Good night, it's heavenly.

You've given us so many blessings, Lord, so many things to enjoy in this life. Help us not to idolize what we have or do. Help us to keep our eyes on the gifts of life and love that you've given us. Strengthen us, we pray, in Jesus' name, Amen.

THE THIRD COMMANDMENT

....

"You shall not misuse the name of the LORD your
God, for the LORD will not hold anyone guiltless
who misuses his name."
—*Exodus 20:7*

She looked up at the pair of rotating fans hung from the peak of the ceiling. "Lots of energy benefits," her father had said, "to having fans up there in church—sound environmental reasons."

He could sound so righteous.

"A couple of ceiling fans will push the hot air back down over us again," he'd said, "and it will keep the air circulating." She remembered how he'd explained it when the Johnsons were over; how he'd said his own company would put them up at cost. "Besides," he'd said, "it'll keep things fresher inside." Sure, keep things fresh in here, she thought. Hot air.

So the church had new fans. Her father always got his way.

"Worthy, worthy, worthy is the Lamb that was slain." She refused to watch him sing the words.

"Your father has such a great voice," her friends said. "Guy, I could listen to him all day. What a great soloist. Aren't you proud of him?"

You want him? You can have him, she thought.

She looked through the list of hymns, an old childhood church game. She tried to see if she could run through all the numbers—one through nine, six numbers, as many as eighteen digits—see if all of them were there. It didn't happen often.

There was no number seven, no number eight. Another failure. So many failures.

You could look the other way, she thought, but you couldn't not listen. No matter how hard you tried to concentrate, you couldn't shut your ears. No matter how hard you tried not to let it hurt, it did. Maybe she should put her fingers in her ears, she thought, stand up and make a spectacle so everyone could see what she thought of her father. Sometimes, she wanted to shout it right from the pulpit—the real truth.

"Worthy, worthy, worthy is the Lamb that was slain."

What possible right does he have, she thought, to be singing about Christ? What possible right does he have to act as though God means so terribly much to him? Isn't that some kind of sin?

If all these people want to see what this worthy lamb really means to my father, she thought, they ought to come around our house sometime. That's what they ought to do. They ought to see what he's like, really—this big-time Christian. "Oh, he sings so nice!"

He was finishing now. You could always tell by the music—when it gets really emotional, you know he's about finished. Thank goodness.

She stared up at the organ pipes, then followed the line of the cross down to just above his head and closed her eyes, brought her hand up to her face, covered it. She wished she could cry.

Even with her eyes closed she could see him up there, a raging smile over his face, proud, powerful. But it was all an act—she knew as no one else did. She wanted so badly to sing it out as loud as he was singing. *You want an act?—watch my father. It's all fake. He's no more worthy than a worm!* She'd like to sing it, the way he sings.

When it was over, she looked down and pulled together all her strength. She knew that in only a few more seconds he would be next to her, sitting there like a loving father. Like the loving father he wasn't. She had listened to him ranting and raving at her and her mother often enough. She had absorbed enough of his foul-mouthed abuse.

Isn't it a sin, somehow—isn't it? Doesn't God even care?

....

Forgive us when our actions don't match our words,
Lord. Forgive us for acting like saints while we live as
sinners. May our lives bring thanks
to your name. Amen.

THE FOURTH COMMANDMENT

"Remember the Sabbath day by keeping it holy. Six days you shall labor and do all your work, but the seventh day is a Sabbath to the LORD your God. On it you shall not do any work, neither you, nor your son or daughter, nor your manservant or maidservant, nor your animals, nor the alien within your gates. For in six days the LORD made the heavens and the earth, but he rested on the seventh day. Therefore the LORD blessed the Sabbath day and made it holy."
—Exodus 20:8-11

It wasn't just the money. True, the money was great. You could make more as a caddy in one day than you could in a whole week of flipping burgers. But it wasn't just the bucks he was after. He'd caddy even if it paid half as much. He just loved golf.

Everybody knew Blair at this course. His parents had a membership, and he'd been out there since he was ten. Shoot, his name was on the plaque in the pro shop for the hole-in-one he'd shot last year—number thirteen, 158 yards, across water, with a seven iron. Right in the cup— he'd never forget it. Ball rolled right in the cup, like it had eyes.

The job application in his hand had a blank at the bottom—*Any special considerations we need to know about.* He knew he had to write it. He really had to. His parents would never let him do it.

So he did. He wrote, "I can't work on Sunday." Then he walked across the office.

Jerry looked out and signaled him to come in. "Blair," he said—everybody knew him at the course.

Jerry took the application and pointed at the chair across the desk. "What do you think?" he said. "You like the way we enlarged the trap on thirteen? We're getting all kinds of flack about it. People say it was already a tough hole."

"As long as you hit the green, you're all right," Blair said.

"Not everybody plays like you do," Jerry told him, looking over the application.

On the walls of the office hung all kinds of pictures of great golfers, signed pictures. You caddy, Blair thought, and you pick up lots of tips. You can learn from the really good guys.

"If you work here your schedule wouldn't change a whole lot," Jerry said, smiling. "Seems like you've been at the course most every day for the last couple of summers anyway."

"I love golf," Blair said.

"You're a good kid," Jerry told him. "Three weeks, you'll be sixteen?"

"The twenty-fifth," Blair said. "May 25."

Jerry smoothed out the ends of his mustache. "Says here no Sunday work, eh?"

Blair nodded.

Jerry raised his eyebrows. "I don't have to tell you that Sunday's the big day around here—you know that. During the week, we don't need caddies all that much. It'd be good to have you around. I mean, I can find other work for a kid like you. You're a good kid. But if you want to caddy, you're going to have to work on Sundays," he said, grimacing. "How stiff is your old man about this?"

"Stiff," Blair said.

"No kidding?"

Blair nodded.

"I'd love to have you," Jerry told him. "Boy, I'd love to have you. But there are lots of kids, you know. I got applications coming out of my ears. I got to figure what works best here too, you know?"

That was it. Blair knew it was over.

"Listen, I'll call you if anything comes up," Jerry said.

Why did it have to hurt so much? Blair thought as he pumped his bike home. Why did being a Christian have to cost so much? Why did it have to hurt so bad?

It wasn't the money either. It wasn't just the money.

....

Dear Lord, help us to do what's right. Give us wisdom to choose obedience, especially when what we choose against looks so right. Help us to be obedient to you every day of our lives. Amen.

THE FIFTH COMMANDMENT

....

*"Honor your father and your mother, so that you
may live long in the land the* LORD *your God is
giving you."*
—Exodus 20:12

I had no idea what Blair's problem was. It never dawned on me that
being a caddy would mean he'd have to work Sundays. Call me stupid,
I guess, but it never even crossed my mind.

When he came up the driveway, I could tell he was battling something major. You can always tell with Blair. He doesn't yell, never talks
back, but when something's wrong, he sulks—gets real dark, like a
dangerous sky.

"So when do you start?" I asked him. Stupid of me, not to think of
what might have happened. I was absolutely sure he'd get the job.

Of course, he didn't say anything. He leaned his bike up against the
wall of the garage. Stood there while I put gas in the Lawn Boy.

"Blair," I said. "You got the job, didn't you?"

I tell you, the look he gave me right then—if there'd been any powder in his stare, he'd have blown me away. Then he headed for the
house.

"Hey," I said, "what's the problem?"

He stopped at the step to the side door.

"You didn't get it?" I said.

I've got to hand it to him for even talking to me. Some kids, I suppose, wouldn't have spit it out—not even if they were asked.

"I can't work on Sundays," he said.

What do you say to your own child? The trouble is, I was pretty sure
it wasn't that he *wouldn't* work on Sunday. I mean, he didn't tell Jerry
that he wouldn't work because of his *own* beliefs. He *couldn't* work. He
turned down the chance to caddy because of us, because of how *we*
feel about working on Sunday. It took me about a second and a half to
figure out that it was me who was in trouble. But what do you say?

"What difference does it make?" he said. "The whole world plays
golf on Sunday. You think if I don't caddy, people will say what a good
Christian I must be—is that it, Dad?"

"It's got nothing to do with what people say," I told him. "I couldn't care less what people say."

"I think it's stupid," he said. "I think it's really dumb. You think God's going to care if I don't go to church much this summer?"

"Yeah," I said.

He rolled his eyes.

"Jerry thinks it's dumb," he said. "He asked me, 'How stiff is your dad about this?'"

"What'd you tell him?"

"Stiff," he said. "'Cause you are."

"That's right," I said. "I am stiff."

"How come?"

"'Six days shall you labor and do all your work,'" I said. "Your mother and I believe, Blair, that it's right *not* to work on Sunday. We believe that verse is meant for us."

He shook his head.

I was surprised, I guess, that on his own he'd told Jerry he couldn't work. But I was happy he had. "Blair," I said, "thanks a lot for what you did."

"What?" he said.

"For respecting me—thanks for respecting what your mother and I believe in. I know it's rough. Thanks."

Then he went into the house. I had thought about making him do the lawn. But I figured maybe this time I'd do it myself.

Lord, respecting parents—no matter how old they are—can be such a chore sometimes. Help us to understand them and to understand the way they've learned to see you. Give us the love to respect them always. In Jesus' name, Amen.

THE SIXTH COMMANDMENT

....

"You shall not murder."
—Exodus 20:13

No one really remembers anymore—no one except my husband and me. Of course, it's been twelve years. I guess I can't expect anyone else to remember. After all, as they say, Jennifer is only a memory now.

To most people.

Weeks can go by without us thinking about it—I mean as husband and wife. But not a day passes without her crossing my mind. I remember the time, about four years ago, when I decided I'd simply keep track for a day of how often I thought about her.

We have one of those magnetic notepads on the refrigerator at home. And at work, of course, I have an appointment book. So I scratched a mark in the book at work, the way prisoners do on walls. Just one little mark for every time I thought about Jennifer.

At home, I marked that magnetic notepad. And by the time Duane and I went to bed that night—it was just past eleven—I counted them up. Fifteen times at work, and another twelve at home. Twenty-seven times, in what—fifteen or sixteen hours? And that wasn't even all of them.

Like I said, sometimes weeks go by

without her death coming up in our conversation, but then something happens—maybe a news story from Atlanta, where she was murdered. All I have to do is hear the word *Atlanta*, and I look up at Duane. I can be lost in a novel or doing some stuff from the office, and when the TV news reporter says, "Atlanta," I'm right there with him at the strip mall.

She was coming out of a discount store. She was working as a social worker down there, a year out of college; trying to make a difference, really. And she'd run in to get a hair dryer. Hers had given out. She picked one up quickly, walked out, and that guy stopped her right at the car—told her he wanted money.

She should have given it to him, I suppose. But all day long she worked with people like him, so she tried to talk him out of it. She just refused.

So he shot her. Killed her. Then he robbed her. Thirteen dollars and some odd change. That and a life sentence—that's what he got.

Our lives have never been the same.

You think you're pretty smart; you think you've arrived. You have a good job, you work hard. And then something happens—you lose a child that way, and it's just as if you've never really lived before. You've never understood how quickly life can change completely.

Today's the anniversary of her death. You know, we visited that strip mall where she was murdered. We were down there to go through the little apartment she'd rented, to go through her things. Both of us wanted to see it. I don't know why—maybe just to be sure that she was dead.

We went there, Duane and I, and people were going in and out. And you know what made me bawl? None of them even seemed to care. A mother came out jerking her crying daughter along. People coming and going.

That man took our child's life—and along with it, a part of ours. It wasn't just Jennifer he killed. He murdered something of me—he really did. Something of both of us. Life is so precious.

Life seems so cheap, Lord. In our world, murders don't even make the front page anymore. Help us to respect life in every way. Help us to build each other up, instead of tearing each other down. Give us strength to fight hate. Help us to love as your Son loves us. Amen.

THE SEVENTH COMMANDMENT

··

"You shall not commit adultery."
—*Exodus 20:14*

I don't know what to do. I mean, I don't know if I should tell some-body, or what. You grow up thinking that a snitch is a snitch, that somebody who turns in a buddy is a real lowlife.

But I don't know what to do.

See, Jason's got this thing about—you're not going to believe this—but he's got this thing about torching his parents' cottage. That's right. You think I'm pulling your leg, but I'm not. I'm serious. I'm dead seri-ous. So is he.

He's planning it, I swear. He tells me this stuff because he trusts me. He tells me because he's got to talk to somebody, I suppose, and I've been his friend for years. We're old buddies, really. But nothing's been the same since his parents broke up.

You know, we both have other friends who've been through this too. But I never saw a case like Jason's. Not really.

Before his old man ran off with that other woman, they used to go to this cottage up north—their cottage. It was a big deal. Every year, they'd catch lots of walleye and bass. You should see Jason's room—he's got pictures all over of him holding stringers full of fish, big heavy lines full. For a while he was really into making his own lures. He makes beauties. The guy loves the outdoors, and he and his old man—they were inseparable. Big time fishermen.

He never expected what happened. I know kids who saw it coming, and they don't have it so bad. But for Jason—the split came right out of the blue. His mom says to him one day—his little sisters, too, they were all sitting there—she says, "Your father wants a divorce."

"How come?" Jason says.

"Because he loves someone else."

This is what he told me exactly. At that point, he says, he didn't even have any idea what his mom meant. He says his little sisters sat there on the couch as if they just wanted to watch TV. He says none of them really understood anything—not until his father stopped coming home altogether. He quit on his wife, and he quit on his kids too.

We saw his father once, the two of us, at the mall. He was with this other woman. Jason ducks into The Gap, and I follow him. "What're you afraid of him for?" I asked him.

"I'm not afraid of him," he says, "I just hate him so much."

I didn't know what to say.

And now he's got this cabin on his mind, see? He thinks he's going up there—I'm supposed to go along—and he's going to torch it. He's going to burn it down. I'm serious.

Jason's crazy. I know he is. But I don't know what to do about it. I tell him it's a nutso idea, but it's in his head, and it doesn't go away. It's like a disease. It's all he thinks about.

I ask him what good is it going to do? And he just looks at me as if I'd never understand.

So what am I supposed to do? Quit being his friend? It seems to me that he needs me now more than ever.

I see what his father did to him, and I just want to be sick. I don't know if I hate him as much as Jason does, but it's like my old friend can't even smile anymore. That's what he's done.

What I want to know is—is love that big a deal that it can destroy your own kids? Maybe you have to be mature to understand. I don't know.

All around us marriages are breaking up, Lord.
Most often, we don't even understand why. Help us
to be faithful to our promises. We know what kind
of sadness a broken marriage creates. Be with those
who hurt because their mom or dad has gone.
Forgive us all our sins. In Jesus' name, Amen.

THE EIGHTH COMMANDMENT

....

"You shall not steal."
—*Exodus* 20:15

I've been at **Bargain Way** for almost a year, and already I'm up to third in seniority among the other part-timers. I mean, people leave that place as if it's thick with radiation. Really.

Minimum wage. After you've worked for five weeks, they say, you get a raise. Sure, a nickel. You could work there forever and not make enough money for an afternoon's supply of Dr. Pepper. I'm not kidding.

I tried to get into Luxembourgs, but it's tough. They treat their help right, so people don't quit like they do at Bargain Way. I mean, the only way people quit Luxembourgs is if they die.

At Bargain Way you never get a break. I work four till eight four nights a week, sometimes a little extra on weekends—men's clothing. Never a dime's worth of overtime. Slave labor is what it is.

The thing is, nobody cares. The guys I work for—shoot, they don't give a rip what happens to the store. Nobody does.

Luxembourgs has Christmas parties for the staff every year. Sometimes the employees get little bonuses and stuff too. Bargain Way—are you kidding? Cheap city. Rip-offville.

So I figure I've got it coming. I mean the merchandise here—it's like eighth rate. Wash a T-shirt once, and your baby brother can't wear it. No kidding. The jeans are as thin as toilet paper.

Who shops here? Only welfare moms and bag ladies. That's it. We don't see people with real money—nothing but food stamps and a government check. No class.

I figure if I wear clothes from Bargain Way it's almost like advertising the place. Shoot, people buy T-shirts all the time that say *Nike* or *Button Your Fly*. If I wear Bargain Way T-shirts—even if they don't say *Bargain Way* on them—I figure it's like free advertising for the store. Who cares that I stole them? Nobody has to know that.

And besides, there's nothing to it. I mean, if they really tried to police the place, it would be one thing, but it seems like nobody even cares.

I'm serious. How do they expect me to give a toot when nobody else does? You hear what I'm saying?

I just take shirts and stuff, mostly. I wouldn't wear their jeans if somebody gave them to me. Now and then some earrings for my girl. Once a watch, but I really needed that.

Listen, if I worked at Luxembourgs, I wouldn't do it. I mean, I'd care.

It's so easy that it's not even like stealing, really. Listen, when we come up short for the night, we just write it off. You know, shoplifting is like this horrendous problem. You wouldn't believe what we lose in a week, really. People are pigs sometimes.

So if I take a shirt home or something, I just scratch it up to all the sticky fingers that come marching through here, you know? The only people who shop here are the Who's Who at small claims court, anyway

See, I got it coming. I figure you got to take what you can in this world or some big guy'll roll right over you.

I got a right to this stuff, and as long as it's not, you know, really big—I mean, not like a CD player or something—I figure nobody's the worse for wear. All we do is write it off.

It's that easy. Nobody cares—nobody. So who's getting hurt? Answer me that. Shoot, just write it off.

....

Lord, it's easy to rationalize our wrongs. Somehow
it feels so much better if we find ways to excuse
ourselves for what we know—inside—isn't
right. Help us respect others—and what
others own. Help us to love, like you
did, even when it's not easy. Amen.

THE NINTH COMMANDMENT

....

"You shall not give false testimony
against your neighbor."
—Exodus 20:16

I'm fifteen, no kid anymore, and I get tired of people talking to me as if I were seven. You expect it of teachers, but not friends.

So we're standing by the lockers yesterday, and I'm trying to put some new tape up on a poster. We've still got four, five minutes to get to class. Tony's standing there, saying nothing.

First hour is algebra. My assignment is done and everything, but I'm still on edge because I hate it when Felton calls on me. Half the time, even though I've got an answer, I'm not at all sure of it. Not like Tony. The minute he gives an answer he rolls his eyes, like the whole high school, Felton included, is dumber than nails.

But that's what Tony's about—he jabbers. He's always jabbering.

"What a jerk," he says, pointing with his thumb at Scott Radeens.

I figure it's jealousy since Scott's got more metal on his letter jacket than Tony's got in the bank. See, wherever Scott walks he's always got eight guys around him, like groupies. He's tough. Probably been shaving since he was four.

So I say to Tony, "Why don't you lift weights or something? Anybody can be a jock. Doesn't take a mind—just pork."

I'm emptying my books into the locker, see, and I haul out my gym bag, which I forgot to take home for the thirty-sixth time this year.

"I never want to be a jock," he says.

"Then why do you let a guy like that bug you?" I ask.

Then he like pours his eyes into mine, as if way down at the bottom of his soul is some dirty secret, and the only path down there is through the black holes of his pupils.

"It's not polite to stare," I say to him.

"It's not polite to do a lot of stuff," he says.

"What'd I do now?" I ask.

"*You* didn't do nothing," he says, smirking.

"Okay, what'd *you* do now?"

"*I* didn't do nothing either."

"What'd Scott do now?"

Boom. Legendary silence. He stands there like a city park statue and expects me, I guess, to figure out some secret he knows.

"What am I supposed to do," I say, "wait for the evening news?"

He starts singing "Good Morning, Sunshine," like it's my wake-up alarm or something. I hate that.

"What's the news, Tony?" I ask. "It's time for class."

"I ain't saying nothing, man," Tony tells me. "All I know is, he goes with your sister."

"So what?" I say.

"So you better keep Kleenex up your ears, brother, 'cause you don't want to know." That's what he says. Then he's off to class, like he can't be late. Walks right away from me—high stepping, too.

It bugs me, all right? And right away I'm thinking the worst—about my own sister too. Can't get my mind off it.

Ten minutes later we're in algebra and Felton, all of a sudden, asks me what I have for number five.

"What page are we on?" I ask.

"Good morning, Arnie," Felton says, and the whole class roars.

I can't help it—she's my sister, after all.

....

Lord, grant us the ability to speak the truth always.
Lying, cheating, stealing—come too easily to us.
Keep us straight with your love. Help us to be
obedient. In Jesus' name. Amen.

THE TENTH COMMANDMENT

....

*"You shall not covet your neighbor's house. You
shall not covet your neighbor's wife, or his
manservant or maidservant, his ox or donkey, or
anything that belongs to your neighbor."*
—*Exodus 20:17*

"Lassiter Pitches Two-Hit Shutout."

You see the headline? Shoot, it's not enough he got all-conference in basketball. He can sing, he can get just about any girl in school, and now we find out he can pitch too. Two-hitter. Big deal. Probably played some rag-arm, wimp team.

Big man, big popular guy. Everybody thinks Lassiter's a pretty nice guy—plus he's got all the talent in the county. I hate it. Makes me sick.

At least my old man is richer than his. Shoot, the day I turned sixteen I had a Camaro in the driveway. Jet black. Picked it out myself. My parents will buy me anything to keep me happy. All I have to do is whine a little, and they come through.

But Lassiter—if he wants to take Emily out, he's got to take his old man's station wagon. Big as a hearse, I'm not kidding. They don't have a garage either, so it's always full of bird dirt.

Brad Lassiter. So what if Emily's got the hots for him? I say, most girls in school would much rather take off in my Camaro than Brad's old man's rust-bucket.

So who wants Emily anyway? Stuck-up priss. Thinks she's God's gift to Emerson High because she's nailed Brad Lassiter. Got herself the all-conference hunk, so now she's all smiles. I hate her. Man, do I hate her!

When I see her in school I just turn around and walk the other way—really. Anybody with a snoot full of pride like hers—I mean, there's no rule you got to talk to somebody like that.

Besides, I'd have tried out for baseball too if I'd had the time. I've got to work, you know. Need the bucks. Got to keep the Camaro running. Games are for kids. I know I'd have made it, too—Coach even asked me to come out, but I told him I didn't have the time.

I used to pitch in Legion ball too, back when Brad Lassiter was just a twink. He was all right, but you know how little he was in seventh grade? I'm not kidding, he was a mite. Pipsqueak.

Back then Emily would have gone out with me, I'm sure. Back then she wouldn't have been so wild about Brad Lassiter. What happened anyway? Brad Lassiter grows up and the whole world suddenly falls over backwards for him. Makes me sick.

You really can't trust a guy like that. I mean, anybody who looks that good on the outside—he's got to have some problem. He's hiding something, I'll tell you. Nobody's perfect, man. There's something rotten in him. Got to be.

Honor role too—National Honor Society. I don't remember him being so smart when we were younger. Emily was always smart, but Brad—he was just a twirp. I think Emily gives him answers.

Really, he's not that smart. Maybe he's the prince of jocks in our school, but upstairs—he's not that sharp.

Emily keeps his grades up, you can bet on it. Stinking cheater.

Everybody's got a weak spot somewhere. Nobody's perfect, man. Shoot, the guy's got everybody just wowing, but she's got to be holding him up. You ever see a jock with brains? No way.

Cheating—and the car. Who'd take out Emily Seavers in an old Dodge station wagon? You got to be out of your mind. I hate him.

Why doesn't he just leave town or something? Make my life easier.

----

*There's always someone who has it better than we
do, Lord. There's always someone who has more
clothes, a better car, or more athletic ability. Help us
to be satisfied with the many blessings you give to
us. Help us not to covet what others have.
In Jesus' name, Amen.*

DON'T DO THIS! DON'T DO THAT!

....

Read Exodus 20:18-21

Curiosity may well have killed a cat or two. Even worse, it threatens most of us most every day. And it was the undoing of Adam and Eve. Think of it this way: The Lord gives Adam and Eve sole ownership of a sprawling national forest. "It's paradise," God says. "Do what you want with it. But remember one little thing. There's this one scraggly fruit-bearing tree out in the wilds somewhere—don't touch it, you hear? Don't even get near it, or you're in big trouble."

Now really, can you blame Adam and Eve for fooling around? I mean, the rest of the woods was bound to get boring eventually. Why should this one bush be out of bounds? Can you blame them for snatching a bite?

Yes, you can. They disobeyed God. It's that simple, no matter what their motives, or how understandable.

God's commandments to the Israelites—we've just gone through the list—can come off the same way to us: "Don't do this, don't do that; don't even think about it." God with a pointy finger.

Oh, yeah, we say, why not? What's so bad about heisting a T-shirt from a third-rate store? Where's the crime in a little fooling around? Sin seems so exciting. Love scenes on TV nearly always take place between people who aren't married. Why not? Marriage is boring, isn't it? Adultery? Wow! Hot stuff! Sneaky love is much more passionate—right?

For some of us, the commandments make sin look dangerously delicious. "Why can't I commit adultery? Let me just try."

But for others, those same commandments create great fear because they're so dreadful—"No, no, no, no."

Maybe the commandments would sound better if they were all stated in a positive way, like the ones about honoring parents and keeping the Sabbath. Wouldn't it be easier to hear, "Honor life," instead of "Thou shalt not kill"?

The commandments can sound so depressing, so negative that listening to them can fill us with trembling. "Don't do this, don't do that!"

Yikes, if that's the way it is, I'm not even going outside the basement for fear I'll do something wrong. "Be careful little eyes what you see!"

That's how the Israelites felt when Moses announced the commandments. They were scared almost to death. "We'd rather not see God again;" they told him, "it's too dreadful. In the future, you go off by yourself and communicate with God, Moses. How does that sound? You be the one that stands between us and God."

The Israelites' fear of God was quite a normal human response, actually. And God honored their request for a mediator—first with Moses, and then later on in the story, with Jesus Christ, the Son of God.

But Moses' response to the people arouses our curiosity here, I think. "Don't be afraid," he tells them. "All these commandments show in pure living color that God is with us. No matter how much these 'don't do this and don't do that' rules make you tremble, remember that they'll keep you from moving away from God, from disobedience. God's rules are a gift of love to you."

Those rules—like the rules set by any good parents—are meant for us to grow. They're discipline for God's disciples. No matter how you read them, God's rules show *love* for us. And that, remember, is positive—or maybe I should say, "Don't forget—that's positive!"

> *Lord, thank you for your law. Help us to see that in this code of behavior lie happiness and joy and satisfaction with life. Help us to see that your laws are really rules to live by. Thank you for your love. Amen.*

OVEREXPOSED

....

Read Exodus 20:22-26

I've been reading lately about Adolf Hitler and art. That's weird, you say. Who'd care to read about that? I do. It's interesting.

You'd think old Adolf would have put tight clamps on paintings and sculptures that picture people stark naked, wouldn't you? After all, Mr. Mustache was hardly a free spirit.

Actually, he rather liked nakedness—and not just in private either. He thought it was wholesome for the German people to enjoy naked men and women in their art, largely because he believed artistic nakedness showed the superiority of the German people and the Aryan (white) race.

One catch, of course. None of the pictures or statues of naked men or women he admired portrayed his fat old Aunt Edna or beer-bellied Uncle Rudolf—no siree. The only nakedness he had in mind was that of statuesque blondes—young men and women with perfect "ten" bods.

Not even an artist like Van Gogh could turn Aunt Edna's nakedness into a work of art. Anybody who's been to a draft physical—better yet, anybody who's ever taken a physical education class—knows very well that in terms of beautiful bods, we are simply not all created equal. There are tons of ugly people in the world, and if they all doffed their clothes the doughy ravages of depravity would be even more apparent.

But let's get back to art. In all of Shakespeare, there's only one nude scene. It's in *King Lear,* and the naked one is Lear himself, the guy who did wrong by giving up the throne when he shouldn't have. Shakespeare intends Lear's nakedness to be ugly, not beautiful. Lear stumbling around naked and blind is a picture of a human being who's been totally humiliated.

I remember studying *Lear* at Arizona State University when an activity called "streaking" was all the rage. Now, streaking wasn't really something new—guys have dared each other to run buck naked from one dormitory to another since way back when. But at that time the fad of streaking got to be a big deal. It was simple—take off your clothes and run somewhere publicly.

Once, I came out of a class where I had just been studying *King Lear* (nakedness = ugliness) and encountered streakers—not all male, by the way—in front of the Language and Literature Building. You know what I thought? Shakespeare had it right. There are only a few models for Michelangelo's "David"—I'll tell you that much. Only a few.

Our meditations for the last while have been rather sober, so it's time to shake out a few laughs. Today's last verse is priceless, isn't it? "Do not go up to my altar on steps, lest your nakedness be exposed on it." The Israelites had never heard of boxer shorts.

I think it's okay to laugh when you read the Bible, even though I'm also sure the prohibition Moses lists here—directed by God—isn't meant to be some kind of Jay Leno rib tickler.

In fact, it's important to remember that these laws God handed to Moses—and the ones still to be read—are deadly serious. Nothing—not human silliness or nakedness—should detract from God's holiness.

God is serious about us. And this last prohibition reminds us that God demands a similar seriousness from us. After all, the Lord is still God. Thanks to God's goodness, we are still God's people—fat or thin, tens or twos—no matter how we're packaged.

No human being can keep on loving the way you do, Lord, That you would stay with us after the many times we've neglected you is a miracle. Help us to respect your holiness, the fact that you are God. And help us to give thanks daily with our lives. Amen.

SLAVERY AND THE PEOPLE OF GOD

....

Read Exodus 21:1-11

Alex Haley died just recently. Chances are you've heard his name before because, twenty years ago, a television program he wrote became one of the most watched shows of all time. That made-for-TV movie, drawn from Mr. Haley's book of the same name, was titled *Roots.*

The story of *Roots* was important to me as a writer. When I saw it, I became very interested in discovering my own roots. *Sign of a Promise,* my first book, is my own "roots" story. But those who benefitted most from the *Roots* saga were, undoubtedly, North America's African-Americans.

Even if you never saw the movie or read the book, you already know, I'd guess, that the "roots" Mr. Haley investigated grew specifically out of African-American history—not Dutch (like mine) or Irish or Jewish. And at least one reason for the incredible popularity of Haley's *Roots* is that no other story of American slavery ever hit people with such force. Kunte Kinte became a household name.

I remember very well, as a white man, being ashamed to the core of my soul by what white people had done to African-Americans—even though my own ancestors never owned a slave and never would have. (My ancestors deliberately stayed away from the American South because when they came over from the Netherlands, they wanted absolutely nothing to do with what they recognized as an evil system.)

No matter. *Roots* made the horror of slavery terrifyingly vivid to anyone with white skin, as well as to Americans of color. No one who saw that movie could deny that slavery—using human beings as if they were nothing more than cattle, property to be used and sold—was evil.

As North Americans, the story of slavery is a regrettable part of our history. I'd rather not talk about it myself, especially since in many cases slaveholders were good, church-going people who didn't even question, apparently, the evil institution they were part of. In fact, some slaveholders used the Bible to condone what they were doing—even passages like this one.

Now all of that history—our history—makes it difficult for us to look at today's passage, a passage in which God Almighty sets out strict and specific laws to govern slavery. You read these laws and you wonder why on earth God didn't simply outlaw the whole ugly business. "If a man sells his daughter as a servant, she is not to go free as menservants do." That's plain awful.

What we need to remember is that there are different types of slavery. You will note that this section has to do with Hebrew slaves. You see, in Israel, people in real debt sometimes offered themselves up into slavery simply to get by. Hebrew slaves were not ripped from their homes the way African slaves were ripped from theirs. Some Hebrew slaves—most of them, in fact—were slaves by choice. No African-American I know of has ancestors who volunteered for slavery.

What these odd regulations actually do is provide a kind of justice—they set some guidelines. God's law here attempts to make the practice of slavery more humane.

It's hard to swallow, I know. But maybe it helps to see that in this passage God brings some justice where otherwise, quite likely, none would exist.

Even so, after watching *Roots*, these laws are hard to read.

Your laws give us life, Lord, but they also affect the way we live. Thank you for justice, for peace, for love—for the example set in your Son, given for us. May we always work, as Christ did, for what is right, for your kingdom. Amen.

THE PLACE OF THE LAW

....

Read Exodus 21:12-36

I'm going to tell a dreadful story to make a point. Hang in there.

Fred's daughter, Sarah, is fifteen. She hangs out at River Park, and he's not happy about it. Even worse, he suspects that she's often with Tony, a kid he knows is really big trouble—three arrests and he's only sixteen.

One night Sarah doesn't come home. Fred is up at two, worried sick. He paces the house for a while, steaming. Then he gets in his car and heads for River Park.

It's dark, except for the shimmer of the moon on the wide river's flow. It seems to Fred that no one's there. He heads down toward the pavilion on the other side of the pines because he knows that's where the kids usually hang out. Slowly his eyes adjust to the darkness, and he searches, listening for any kind of sound.

He sees signs of some-one's presence—beer cans and fast food wrappers—all around. Cigarette butts litter the cement around the three picnic ta-bles.

Then he hears moaning from behind a stone grill. He finds his daughter sprawled on the ground, incoherent. Her clothes are shredded and she's covered with blood, close to death.

Fred is overwhelmed, and then enraged. Hands fisted, he screams.

Once he gets his daughter to the hospital, chances are Fred will want to take off after Tony. I'm not sure what he'll do if he catches him.

Laws exist for many reasons, I suppose. At least one of those reasons is to contain Fred's thirst for revenge—the Fred that's in all of us. If it weren't for the law, Fred might take a chain saw to Tony without stopping first to consider whether Tony was, in fact, responsible for what happened to Sarah. After all, it's entirely possible he wasn't.

When we read today's long recitation of laws we need to remember that the Israelites had been living in captivity for hundreds of years. Their only laws—for getting along with each other, for "doing justice"— were the laws of the Egyptian slaveholders.

After living through incredible plagues and walking through the Red Sea's dry bed, the Israelites still knew very little about living together. And certainly, for some of the Israelites at least, memories of the God of Abraham had faded. For them, everything about this experience was new. They found themselves following a leader whose mountain quaking God many of them didn't even recognize.

The laws we're looking at establish standards that are not only useful but also essential for making a society work. Ask people from Liberia what life is like without law—it's chaos, anarchy. Without the law, people have nowhere to turn for relief, for justice, for protection.

Some of the laws God handed to Moses for the Israelites may seem strange to us, thousands of years later. But they were absolutely essential to a people wandering in the desert under circumstances they'd never even considered just a short time ago.

Finally, the law points at values—the standards by which people should live. It's God, the lawgiver, who establishes those values—for the Israelites and for us today.

Okay, the laws may seem strange. But they're necessary. Always.

....

*Dear Lord, your law brings life. Thank you
for your Word. Amen.*

MY PROPERTY

....

Read Exodus 22:1-15

In the neighborhood where I grew up, we used to get into fights. Mostly, I think, because we wanted each other's stuff—baseball gloves, roller skates, bikes, squirt guns. You know, coveting.

Here's what happens: I grab the neighbor kid's plastic Luger, fill it from the outside faucet, then drown him with his own merchandise.

The kid gets irritated. Then, spitting mad, calls me a snot-faced dork and lickety-splits it home because he knows he's about to get pounded. So I chase him—to a certain point. Once he gets to his own yard, he stands, bottom lip flattened, and points down to his feet.

"You mayn't come on my propi'ty," he says.

For some reason, I listen. We leer at each other across an imaginary border, glowering, neither of us moving. I'm scared of his mother, who constantly watches over her little honey. So we stand there steaming until somehow we finally settle our differences and get back to serious play.

The laws we've read through today have to do with *property*—what's rightfully mine, and yours. They all deal with damage to property in one way or another—through theft, fire, or breach of trust.

The philosopher Karl Marx believed that most every problem imaginable is rooted somehow in owning personal property. The solution he proposed was a more even distribution of property—that is, a society in which everybody got the same size shovel, pail, and sandbox.

Unless you haven't been in tune with the news in the last few years, you know what happened to his system, communism. It went, as they say, belly-up.

The idea of owning property—not only land but also squirt guns—is important to us, and the laws in today's passage indicate it was important to the Israelites as well. Take my bike, and you'll pay, Abe.

But we can make some interesting observations here. Let's stop for a few specifics.

Observation 1: Isn't it interesting that the first four verses—all of which have to do with stealing—mention no prescribed jail sentence?

Instead, the penalty involves having to repay the loser for what's been taken, in some cases double (v. 4). Don't you wonder what would happen if that were true today?

Observation 2: According to verse two, being robbed at night is a whole lot worse than being robbed during the day. (You don't have to tell that to Hollywood—seen any movies about daytime burglers?) If a man kills a thief breaking into his house at night, no charge; but during the day he can't lay him out and get off scott-free. What's the difference? Is it fear? Probably more significant is the owner's ability, during the day, to figure out whether the thief is after his life or his pole lamp.

Observation 3: Verse five's warning about respecting other people's pastures indicates that these rules weren't intended only for the duration of the Israelites' wilderness wandering. Instead, these are long-term laws, as effective in the desert as they would be in the promised land.

Actually, I think the Lord probably smiled about the way my neighbor kid toed his property line. According to these rules, though, if I'd grabbed the kid's sand pail, I'd owe him all right—and his mother would have seen to it that I paid. She was always watching over him.

....

When we consider how much each of us here in North America really has, it's almost amazing, Lord, that we could ever want more. Help us not to worship our possessions, even when those possessions bring us prestige or popularity or power. It's only in your name that we hold anything at all. You are our God. In your Son's name, Amen.

THE STORY OF GEORGE BURROUGHS

....

"Do not allow a sorceress to live."
—*Exodus 22:18*

George Burroughs had been a great athlete in college. His complexion was dark, even swarthy, and his body, sinewy and strong. He was known for accomplishing feats requiring immense physical strength.

In May of 1692, Burroughs was the pastor of a little church in Maine, miles and miles from the Massachusetts Bay Colony, where he'd once served a church in the town of Salem. Married to his third wife (he'd outlived two others), Burroughs was the father of eight children.

One day a group of men, a posse, came barging into his house completely unexpected. They ripped him away from the table where he had been eating dinner with his family and hauled him off to Salem. Burroughs was given no opportunity to say goodbye to his wife; in fact, he wasn't even allowed to finish his meal. The men had a warrant for his arrest.

Back in Salem, a few young girls from his former congregation had determined that George Burroughs, along with others, had infected them with Satan. George Burroughs, they said, was a witch.

He was brought to Salem on March 4. Four days later he was examined by a jury of his peers, fellow clergymen. Reverend George Burroughs admitted that he hadn't taken communion for some time. Furthermore, he told the jury that only his eldest son had been baptized. Both of these problems made the Massachusetts pastors scowl. But when they questioned him on doctrine, they found less to criticize.

Once their examination was finished, they had Burroughs strip-searched to see if his body bore any toothmarks, a sign of the devil himself. Although they found no unusual marks on his body, the jury noted that his muscles seemed abnormally large.

He was brought before the court, bewildered and shocked by what had so suddenly and inexplicably occurred in his life. He looked about the courtroom, as if to locate a friendly face among the parish he'd once served. He found none.

When the judge ordered him, for the first time, to look directly into the faces of the young women who were his accusers, a horrid shrieking went up. The girls fell to the floor, writhing.

The judge asked his opinion, and Burroughs said, "It's an amazing and humbling providence, but I understand nothing of it."

The testimony brought forward accused him of murder—not physical murder, but "spectral murder," something only felt, not seen. His victims, said the prosecutors, included the white men murdered by Indians in the wilderness where he presently lived, as well as his two previous wives.

The judges heard testimony that Burroughs' physical strength was greater than human strength could be. He had once lifted an entire barrel of molasses with just two fingers, someone said. A sign, certainly, of the devil.

So the former pastor was convicted and sent to prison. And on August 19, 1692, along with fifteen others similarly accused, George Burroughs was hanged.

Before he died, though, he spoke with such sincerity and conviction, it is said, that even those most obsessed with the evils of witchcraft listened and cried. Burroughs maintained his innocence, repeated the Lord's Prayer, and then was killed.

By what law? "Thou shalt not suffer a witch to live."

Lord, sometimes even with the best of intentions, we make big mistakes. When we consider what happened in Massachusetts three hundred years ago, we recognize that good people were dead wrong. In all of our lives, forgive us. We live in the promise that you've given us here in Exodus and elsewhere—that you will. In the name of your Son, Amen.

MY OFFICE-MATE, THE WITCH

....

"Do not allow a sorceress to live."
—Exodus 22:18

I'm not making this up. I once shared an office with a witch, a guy named Marty (not his real name). He didn't cackle, wear a pointy hat, or buzz the streets of Milwaukee on a straw broom.

Marty was a poet, and he told me that he often went to coven meetings. Actually, he was a pretty strange guy; I always thought there was something weird about him. But as far as I know, he never stuck pins in dolls; or mixed toad toes, eagle claws, and turtle eggs into any kind of witching brew. I *hope* he never cursed me.

But Marty was a witch all right. He told me so.

Now, according to the verse we're looking at again today—if I believe what it says to be God's truth—I'm obligated not to let him live, right? I should have come up behind him while we were in the office correcting freshman essays, slipped a noose of baling wire around his neck, and offed him, right?

Wrong. But it's a tough problem. The bigger question here is, what on earth do we do with laws like this one? Do we take them to heart? Should we still practice them? After all, the Bible is the Word of God.

I can offer three options: one of them is easy; two are tough. Let's start with the easy one.

Option 1: We can just write off the whole works. Let's face it, those Israelites were a weird crew. Their bizarre laws just aren't worth a toot today. Once Christ came, everything changed. The whole Old Testament is just so much dusty history that's got nothing at all to do with the here and now.

I don't know about you, but I'm not particularly comfortable with tossing out so much of the Bible simply by calling it irrelevant.

Option 2: All these laws are still valid. Because the Bible is the Bible, we can't just pick and choose which verses we feel like obeying. Therefore, I really should have murdered Marty, even if I had to spend the rest of my life in jail for homicide.

This option appeals to me because it takes the Bible seriously as the Word of God. What I don't like about it—well, you can guess. I'm not really into murder—by stoning, strangulation, or hanging.

Option 3: These laws have to be read within their context, in order to discern their spirit. Some of them have meaning for us today; some simply don't.

Take the laws about slavery, for example. Thank God slavery is a thing of the past in our society. The laws we've already looked at—the ones dealing with slavery—are irrelevant to us because times have changed. The spirit of the law—that slaves need justice too—is still true all right. But the laws themselves are what lawyers call "moot": obsolete, irrelevant.

Now here's the tough part. What about witches? I know we still have witches; remember Marty? Does that mean the law still has to be enforced? Should I have killed the guy?

I hope you agree with me when I say no. We'd all be in big trouble if people like me just up and acted on laws given to the Israelites so many years ago.

Think about this: Anyone who curses his mother or father should be put to death (21:17). Wow. Who's going to do it? The preacher? Your local consistory? By what means? Does she get a trial? Who's to judge?

I told you it was tough. Read on.

....

Sometimes your Word can be confusing, Lord.
Sometimes all of it seems strange. Give us wisdom
to understand what you've given to us in your Son
and in your Word. Help us to live obediently.
Amen.

MAKING SENSE

....

Read Exodus 22:19-31

We've stumbled on a mega-problem here. Do these laws mean anything today or not? If they do, why don't we kill witches, or execute kidnappers (21:16), or lend money without charging interest (22:25)?

I don't want to beat all of this to death, but it really is a tough problem, and, I think, an interesting one. The questions we're asking here go to the very heart of our relationship to this book—the whole holy Word of God.

Yesterday, I told you three different ways we could look at the laws God gave the Israelites. First, shrug them off as if they mean nothing at all to us. Assume they're just so much dead history. Second, believe and practice them all still today. That would mean, of course, that I should have killed Marty, my office-mate. Whoa!

Third, read them wisely. That takes more work.

I know looking at history may not be as exciting as a day at Great America, but sometimes it helps to see what other people have thought about this question.

Take the theologian John Calvin. Calvin outlined three different kinds of Old Testament laws. First, he said, are laws that convince us of sin—like the Ten Commandments. Second are laws that show us gratitude (we haven't come to those yet). And third are ceremonial laws, the ones dealing with day-to-day life among the Israelites.

Ceremonial laws, Calvin said, are shaky at best, because they have to do with the way the Israelites lived thousands of years ago. They have little to do with us. That's not true of the other two categories of laws: we all need to be convinced that we have sinned, and we all need to give thanks.

But what about these others—the ones that are creating problems for us?

The Israelites as a people were still learning about their God. Among their enemies were pagan sorcerers and sorceresses—people who trusted not in the I AM, but in other gods. And pagan ideas were very dangerous to God's inexperienced people.

Let's put it this way. I put up with Marty, my office partner. I didn't kill him. To tell the truth, I don't think my faith is a whole lot worse today for having sat beside him grading papers. I didn't need to cut his throat to save my faith in the Creator God. In fact, Marty knew I was a Christian, and he respected my beliefs.

Times change. That's so obvious one hardly needs to say it, and yet, it's a scary statement. The Bible is not static, and it's not just a book for people long gone. God's Word is a living Word. Our God is the same God of the Israelites, but today, we live in a different world.

When the Puritans used a single verse to justify hanging George Burroughs, they were wrong. They were wrong because times change. When they took that verse to be just as true for them as it was for the Israelites, they missed the spirit of the law—the spirit made visible in the Word made flesh, Jesus Christ.

I wish this were easier. After all, faith itself is very simple—you just believe. But God's Word isn't always so easy.

Just recently I read a poem of Marty's somewhere. He's still alive. It's possible that God may yet save Marty, isn't it?

Even though I didn't carry out one of the laws God gave the Israelites, I think I did the right thing. I really do. My guess is, so do you.

....

We know that your promise to us—your love forever—never changes. We believe that your love for your people was so great that you gave your own Son. Thank you for the gift of faith. Help us to know you better and to grow in your grace. Amen.

FIRSTFRUITS

Read Exodus 22:29-30; 1 Samuel 1

I know that the primary reason Hannah's story is included in the Bible is this: it tells the story—the earliest story—of Samuel, one of the great judges of Israel. Now, I don't have any way to back this up, but I also have a sense that Hannah's story is in the Bible at least partially for another reason—because it's unusual.

I have this sneaking suspicion that when the Israelites sat around their campfires eating s'mores and telling stories, they tended to tell the weird or unusual ones most often—just as we do today. And for that reason, I think Hannah's story came up regularly.

Why not? No stories are quite as satisfying as the ones that present us with really detailed and fulfilling answers to prayer.

Here's Hannah, praying so emotionally that Eli—who should have recognized real drunkenness since his two boys were such rounders—accuses her of being pie-eyed. Here's Hannah, taking putdowns from Peninnah, her rival, for not being able to have kids. Here's

Hannah, feeling woefully empty because God hasn't granted her any children.

So she cuts a deal with God. "Give me a child," she says, "and he's yours." And the Lord listens. Poof! She's pregnant.

As soon as her blessed boy, Samuel, is three, Hannah fulfills her promise to God: she gives him up. She brings Samuel to the temple and gives him to the Lord.

Now, any woman who prayed that hard for a child must have had a hard time giving him up so soon, right? Any other woman, maybe; but not Hannah. She had promised, after all. She'd received her end of the bargain, the child she wanted so badly. And Hannah was enough of a believer to realize that having her child belong to the Lord was itself the most marvelous blessing she could receive. So, she brings the boy the temple—just as she had promised.

It's a great story.

Let's think about Exodus 22:29-30. Did the Lord have Hannah in mind here? Did he expect every woman pregnant with her first child to bring that child to the temple to become a priest? No. After all, who's going to dig potatoes? It's true that the Lord called the Israelites a "kingdom of priests," but that doesn't mean that everyone worked at the temple.

Okay, then what does the passage mean?

It could well mean that the firstborn child had to be brought to the temple for circumcision, since God had instructed the people to be circumcised already back in Genesis 17. It could mean that, but maybe it doesn't.

Now, hold on to your hat. What I'm about to suggest might blow it— or you—away. It could also mean that the firstfruits of the Israelite people were to be brought to the altar for sacrifice. That's right—think the worst. Ouch. But before you throw in the towel on this whole story, let's go slowly. Although it *could* mean that, most Bible commentators don't think so. I'd much rather believe that Hannah's story was only one of a million similar stories, wouldn't you? That giving your firstborn meant dropping him off at the temple?

Even so, some people really do believe that the verse "You must give me the firstborn of your sons" could imply that the Israelites, in those early days, actually sacrificed their babies to God.

Some things we'll likely never know. Just exactly what God intended here might be one such mystery. But there's more to say about this "firstfruits" command, so stay tuned. It won't get worse.

···

It's almost scary, Lord, to think that you really demand our best. It seems as if we give our best to other people, or to school, or to ourselves. Help us to give our best—our lives—to you in thankfulness. In Jesus' name, Amen.

FIRSTFRUITS II

....

Read Exodus 22:29-30; 13:11-16

You'll notice that the Bible reading I've given you today goes backwards. Obviously, I've done that for a reason.

Yesterday, I laid this burden on you: some people think the command given in verse 29 of Exodus 22 implies that the Israelites, like a lot of other desert tribes, actually sacrificed—that is, killed—their babies as an offering to God.

Just in case you didn't read that verse again, let's go over it one more time: "You must give me the firstborn of your sons. Do the same with your cattle and your sheep. Let them stay with their mothers for seven days, but give them to me on the eighth day."

I find it incomprehensible that God would require the death of children as a sacrifice. But how else do we understand this verse?

First, let's look at the other passage I wanted you to read. In verse 12 of chapter 13, God commands the same sacrifice as he does in Exodus 22. But then, in verse 13, he commands the Israelites to "redeem every firstborn among your sons." Here *redeem* means "to obtain release by means of a payment." It seems that what God wanted from the people was sacrifice, all right. God demanded the sacrifice not of a child, but of an animal—a lamb, in this case—for the "redemption" of the firstborn boys.

All of this, of course, for a reason. Verses 14-16 explain that, more than anything, God wants praise—praise that comes from the Israelites' remembering what the Lord has done for them. So the purpose of redeeming firstborn sons was to inspire thanksgiving and praise for the marvelous acts God accomplished in freeing the Israelites from Pharaoh's rule.

Bing, bing, bing! Now if all of this is starting to ring some bells, that's good. We've been on this trail before, and we'll travel it again. "Being saved" from captivity requires a sacrifice. Bing, bing, bing! Sound like a tune you've heard before?

Likewise, our "being saved," our redemption, requires a sacrifice too. Okay, so my ancestors were never slaves in Egypt. But those ancestors, along with all of us, needed to be redeemed from a different kind of slavery. They needed the sacrifice of a different lamb, the "lamb of God."

It's in rather poor taste to quote yourself, but I'm going to do it anyway: "I find it incomprehensible that God would require the death of children as a sacrifice." That's what I wrote just a few minutes ago.

Bing, bing, bing! Are lights turning on now? They should be.

God's own Son was the sacrifice for our redemption—God's child for our sins, Christ's life for our lives. It doesn't seem any less incomprehensible really, does it? And yet, for some of us, maybe because we've heard it—"God so loved the world that he gave his one and only Son"—so often, it's become old hat.

Put it this way: God's Son was laid on the altar to die for God's people. In the same way, God demands firstfruits— our best, our first. He demands our best hockey, our finest masonry, our most perfect sculpture. After all, we first received God's firstfruits, God's own Son.

Sometimes you can read the Bible wrong if you just pick out verses here and there. But if you watch the way it all flows—that's when the lights go on.

Bing, bing, bing!

Things fit. Things flow. They make sense. Alleluia.

Thank you, Lord, for giving us your firstfruits. Amen.

"AH, JUST LET IT GO"

....

Read Exodus 23:1-9

I saw this firsthand—or maybe I should say, "first eye."

Quite a few years ago, my wife and I accompanied a group of young people from our church—mostly young women—to an area of the country where people were really poor. We set up a Vacation Bible School in an old, run-down country church. Kids from little tar-paper shacks came from miles around.

Now, what I'm about to tell you isn't very sweet. But then, we've been reading passages in Exodus that aren't exactly Disney quality either. So here goes.

Boys, people say, will be boys. That's not a sexist statement; it's the truth. Boys can be obnoxious anyway (so can girls), but when the hormones start flowing—if you know what I mean—they can be more than a little forward. (I'm trying to be nice in my choice of words.)

Here's what happened. Some of the boys who hung around our Bible school began getting friendly with the high school girls we brought down to teach the kids. Now there's nothing wrong with friendly, right? Of course not. But these boys—maybe eleven or twelve years old—starting grabbing the girls in places where "hands off" is the best policy, the right policy. Get my drift?

And what did these young women do about it? They smiled politely, even sweetly, waved a hand just a bit, and giggled. No kidding. That's it. They didn't invite the boys to keep on doing it, but neither did they tell them to shove off. They were trying to be nice.

Let me assure you of one thing. If those girls had been back home and their little brothers' buddies tried to pull the kind of grabbing these boys did, they'd have exploded—and they'd have been right to explode. Their reaction wouldn't have been the same at all.

So why did they react differently that summer? It's simple. Because the boys doing the goosing in this run-down churchyard were poor, that's why. The girls didn't scold those boys for their behavior—behavior that was and is flat wrong—for one reason: because the boys were poor.

The Exodus passage for today establishes some standards for justice and mercy. Verse 3 contains a line we sometimes need to be reminded of: "Do not show favoritism to a poor man in his lawsuit." There may have been no lawsuits in the poor town where we worked that summer, but there certainly was behavior that should have been corrected.

Sometimes it seems almost heartless to have to correct someone whose lot in life is so ragged. But God's command to the Israelites was clear: with respect to the truth they were to be as blind as a bat. "Justice is blind," wrote John Dryden; "he knows no man."

And that's the focus of the rest of the verses. Don't let the crowd sway you from doing, and saying, what's right. Don't let the popular people scare you away from doing what's best.

And if your worst enemy lands his Mustang in the ditch (v. 5), for the sake of God's own love, pull him out. That's the right thing to do.

Sometimes doing the right thing can be awfully hard: when you're dealing with a kid who's poor or an outsider (v. 9), when the whole crowd's against you (v. 2), or when someone's offering a little bribe on the side (v. 8).

Justice, says the Lord, is doing the right thing. As glorious as that may sound, anybody who's lived for very long knows it's sometimes really tough. But it's right.

....

It's really easy to let things go when they happen to
our friends, Lord. And it's really easy to blame
others when they're not our friends or our "type."
Help us to do what's right in all cases, not showing
favoritism toward others for any reason. Amen.

BLESSED ASSURANCE

....

Read Exodus 23:10-13

Just a month ago, I sat up in front—where I always sit—for graduation exercises at the college where I teach. Graduations are graduations. Almost the same things happen every year. Even the graduates, in their funny hats and robes, look the same.

But something different happened this year. At the end of the program, the college choir circled the crowd and sang a familiar hymn, "Blessed Assurance." Maybe you know it. It goes like this: "Blessed assurance, Jesus is mine. Oh, what a foretaste of glory divine"—and so forth.

They sang it without accompaniment, and I felt overwhelmed. I nearly cried. It was simply beautiful. It was enchanting. It was exhilarating. I'm sure the rest of the crowd was as thrilled as I was.

All except one guy. (At least, I know of only one.) He's a guy I respect—smart, able, committed, a strong Christian. He thought the song was dumb, and wrong.

Here's why. He claims that music like "Blessed Assurance" lifts us up on the wings of its own beauty, and escorts us out of our life into a heavenly world of perfect harmony. A song like that, he says, relieves us of the burden of working in the world God gave us.

You might remember that in Exodus 19, where God's covenant with Israel is outlined again, the people are told they were chosen to bring glory to God's world—and not necessarily to themselves: "Although the whole earth is mine, you will be for me a kingdom of priests and a holy nation." Don't get a big head, the Lord might have said, you'd better start pumping iron. You've got work to do because the mandate I give is not to strut around the temple but to minister to my world.

My friend feels—and I understand him—that singing songs like "Blessed Assurance" literally gets us high. It gets us weepy and muddle-headed about life, he says, and makes us dream only about heaven. It can be exhilarating, all right, but then, I'm told, so can a good snort of cocaine.

I still like the hymn, but I know what my friend means. Being full of God's grace should never empty us of our concern for God's world.

Today's passage deals once again with Sabbath laws. This time, something like a Sabbath year is included. Every seven years, God says (again, looking ahead to the time the Israelites would be in Canaan), let your land stretch out for a rest.

Why a Sabbath year? God's answer could have been, "Because I said so." But instead the people are given perfectly practical reasons. First, the poor would benefit by gathering extra food from the land left to rest; and second, the wild animals would be able to feast on the leavings. In short, the Sabbath year was good for God's world.

Likewise, the Sabbath day. Why should the Israelites keep it? Because it was important for the upkeep of their animals—not to mention their slaves. "Let everything rest," God tells the people. "Sit back and smell the roses."

I find it interesting that even the Sabbath laws have very practical benefits for God's world. Worshiping and praising God specifically on the Sabbath not only increases our own "blessed assurance" of salvation, it also prompts us to shape up God's world.

God knows that when faith has little to do with day-to-day life, it fails to be faith. And the commandments assure us of that.

My friend might be a little too critical. It's great to be exhilarated sometimes. Just as long as we bring that exhilaration on home to God's world. I still like the song. But I know what my friend means.

....

Give each of us blessed assurance of our salvation,
Lord. Help us to be confident of your promise
to love us forever. Make us instruments of
your peace. Amen.

DOINGS

....
Read Exodus 23:14-19

In the town where I grew up, the American Legion throws a party every Fourth of July—hamburgers, brats, games for the kids, and even a few rides. My grandma used to call it "the doings"—as in, "Hey, what time are you going to the doings?" That's the only time I've ever heard anybody use the expression.

For the kids of Oostburg, Wisconsin, that celebration was, and still is, such a big deal that it almost demands its own word. We'd look forward to it for weeks—the tangy smell of barbecued brats filling the holiday air, John Philip Sousa marches playing all day long, everybody wearing their new summer duds. Big-time good times.

It's been quite a while since I lived in Oostburg, Wisconsin. But my guess is that even today none of the parents have to remind their kids that next month (I'm writing this in June) will be Fourth of July, time for the "doings." Everybody knows. Everybody goes.

In the Scripture passage for today, God commands the Israelites to put on three big parties a year. It's not a suggestion—God demands it.

"Listen," the Lord says, "I'm not giving you a choice here. I'm telling you only once, and I don't ever, ever want you to forget: THREE TIMES A YEAR I WANT PARTIES IN MY NAME, HEAR?"

Some commands are really tough to take.

Actually, this command tells us something about God, I think. For one thing, it suggests that God knows us pretty well. The "doings" in Oostburg's Veterans Park every Fourth of July don't have diddly to do with the Declaration of Independence, George Washington, or the Boston Tea Party. They're all about trying to win a chartreuse teddy bear for your sweetie and finding out who's got the winning ticket for the big raffle prize—a trip to some Holidome in Chicago. And at night the fireworks go off—big booms echo all over the county—but not much is said about the Battle at Bunker Hill or the First Continental Congress.

It's a great party, but you can go to "the doings" for your entire childhood and never know anything about *freedom.*

"Three times a year," God says, "I want you all to get together, and I want you to accomplish certain kinds of 'doings' at these shindigs." God knows town picnics are wonderful, but God also understands us very well—and the fact is, in all the good times, we simply forget.

It's fascinating to realize that this whole exodus story is a really big deal to *God!*

After all, it's easy to understand how the story of their escape from Egypt would be incredibly memorable to the people of Israel. But the command to celebrate the Feast of Unleavened Bread shows very clearly that the Lord's delivery of the Israelites from the clutches of that slave driver, Pharaoh, was no everyday thing. Even to God, the exodus was an epoch-making experience.

Why? This is my idea: delivering the Israelites from slavery was a de-fining event for the Lord God Almighty. For years, the Lord had held back; and then, for a time, God entered into the lives of the Israelites in a unique way—to *show God's identity* as the I AM. Not that the Lord didn't operate in people's lives before, but this time was special, even definitive.

It was important for the Israelites not to confuse the Lord God with silly Egyptian animal gods, and later, in the wilderness, with Assyrian gods. God wanted Israel to know and remember the I AM. The whole exodus story, God seems to imply, is about one thing: WHO I AM. And don't for-get it.

To find out about Michael Jordan, you look at what he does with a bas-ketball. And to find out about the Lord God of Creation, you look at the story of God's people.

Don't ever forget it. Celebrate! Dance to that music.

Thank you for the whole story of the exodus, Lord—
thank you for revealing so much of yourself in what
you did for your people. Thank you for saving grace in
all of our lives. Amen.

DEFINITION

....

Read Exodus 23:20-26

You know, I'm told that some people actually like learning vocabulary. I hate it. When I was a kid, memorizing definitions was just about the only way to learn a foreign language. And the ability to learn languages—just like the ability to do algebra or understand poetry—always seemed to me something you either had by nature, or you didn't have. E=mc²? Okay, I give up.

But now I realize that when we think, we're always giving definitions. Take Professor Discomboobalate, looking through a microscope at all kinds of unrecognizable shapes. What she's doing, of course, is trying to define a certain kind of shape and a certain kind of organism. "Here is de pattern," she says, slipping the glasses back up her nose. "I tink ve got it. Dis is vat an amoeba rrreeeeally is."

I'm no scientist, but when I write stories, I start with something perplexing—maybe a little anecdote, maybe a character. I think and think and think, then write and write and write, until finally something makes sense. *That's what's at the heart of it,* I tell myself. *That's what's really going on here.* I define something.

Definition. If you don't think, you don't define anything. But if you do think, you're always doing it: "So *that's* what it is!"

In yesterday's meditation I said I thought maybe the reason God made such a big deal out of bringing the children of Israel together in yearly festivals was definition. Maybe God was saying, "I don't want you to forget, because what I did for you in Egypt—and what I'm still doing here in the wilderness on the way to Canaan—is giving you a definition of myself. Knowing the exodus = knowing me."

We've now arrived at the end of a section of the book of Exodus that most commentators call "the Book of the Covenant." In chapter 21, verse 1, God tells Moses, "These are the laws you are to set before my people."

Ever since then, we've been reading a code of laws that sometimes makes us chuckle, sometimes wince; nevertheless, a code God wanted the Israelites to take with utmost seriousness.

Why? Here we go again. Definition. The people of Israel needed some kind of code, some body of laws, to structure their lives in the wilderness and beyond. After all, as we've said before, in Egypt they were the victims of the laws of oppressors. But after the exodus, the Israelites were on their own. They needed to know how to live. The laws told them how. "With these laws," God might have said, "I'm defining the kind of life you must live."

And the laws also define God. Nobody really understands God, of course, because only God is God. But the laws show God to be someone who wants to be remembered, who demands that people act justly and show each other humane consideration. In short, they reveal a God who wants people to love each other. The laws define God's own values. They define God.

As does this whole book. Why read the whole Bible? Because it teaches us a way to live. Absolutely. It shows us that faith means action. It spells out plainly how we should live.

But in the process, the Bible also defines God. If we come to see the whole story of the redemption of God's people, then we'll come as close as we'll ever come to understanding the God who made us, and this whole incredible world we live in.

The I AM. The book itself is a big part of how we know God.

....

As we grow older it seems that we understand
more and more about ourselves and even about
you. Thank you for allowing us to learn, for the
gifts of thought and analysis. Grant that we
may use every talent you've given us
for your glory. Amen.

A BIT MORE OF A DEFINITION

....

Read Exodus 23: 27-33

You know how it is: when a certain song gets in your head you sing it for three days, even when you'd rather not.

My kick for the last couple of meditations has been *definition*. The point is this: what we're reading helps us to *define* God.

Using the Scripture passages from yesterday and today, let's just put my idea into practice.

Today's stumper is this: Who in the world is this "angel" God claims to be sending to the Israelites (v. 20)?

Let's define the angel by what the passage says.

- According to verse 20, the angel is coming straight from God. Is God like a military general or an old-fashioned king surrounded by lots of strange beings who hang out and wait for orders? Maybe. God promises to send one of them on a mission.
- Verse 21 tells us that anything this angel says is worth listening to. What's the deal? Does the angel have a mobile phone?
- The same verse also says the angel won't forgive the Israelites if they just shrug off his orders. Really? Does God allow the angel to make up his own mind about things?
- Also according to verse 21, the angel has the badge of the Lord God: "My Name is in him." Is the angel a part of God, or what?
- According to verse 22, this angel speaks with God's own voice. Watch the way the verse uses pronouns: "If you listen carefully to what he says and do all that I say, I will be. . ." It seems this angel is not just some lieutenant with a chest full of medals; rather, this angel actually speaks with God's own voice.

What does all of this mean? Well, if we check through other passages, we see that God leads his people in different ways: through a pillar of cloud some of the time (ch. 13), and on a later occasion, through the ark of the covenant (Num. 10). In chapter 14, verse 19, we see that the angel of the Lord was already around: "Then the angel of God, who had been traveling in front of Israel's army, withdrew and went behind them."

My daughter works at the Dairy Queen downtown. Now, we live in Sioux Center, Iowa, which is hardly a high crime spot, but my wife says that sometimes when Andrea has to close up the DQ, she worries about Andrea walking home alone. What my wife—like lots of parents—would like to be able to do is create an angel of her own to walk our daughter home through the evil darkness of late-night Sioux Center. Unfortunately, she lacks that ability. We can't just send out parts of ourselves to supervise our children. It would make a great movie, but it's just not possible.

Obviously, though, God can. In fact, God can become a burning bush. And in Judges 6, the Lord sent prophets special delivery when the people needed them.

I've got it. God must be something like a *plannaria,* a little flatworm, genus *Bugesia.* Remember? You cut them in pieces, and all the pieces become separate little squiggly flatworms. One of the most amazing experiments in tenth-grade biology.

Wrong. The burning bush is not a separate God. Neither is the angel God promises to send to the Israelites, or the prophets. These little bits of God don't become separate deities.

So what do we know? What does all of this tell us about God? Amazingly, this: that God can decide to act in our lives. God has done it before and will do it again.

Bing, Bing, Bing! Does that ring any bells? It will.

....

An idea like the Trinity is very difficult to
understand, Lord. But we know that you are God,
and that you can do all sorts of things we humans
can't. We thank you for your Spirit, Lord, and we
thank you for your Son. And for the angels
you bring us, even when we don't even see
them sometimes. We thank you that you
are our God. Amen.

PROMISES, PROMISES

Read Exodus 23:24-33

Jenny's a good kid—works hard on the school paper, gets decent grades, has lots of friends, is rarely rowdy.

But one night not long ago, she got smashed. She and her friends found a bottle of vodka in Stephanie's house and demolished it in a half hour. None of them had ever drank anything before, so they thought they'd experiment, check out what a buzz was really like.

Boy, did they get walloped. First they laughed, they roared, they screamed, they had a ball. Then they got sick—we're talking infirm here, each, in turn, lurching toward the bathroom throne.

Jenny had it the worst.

The others got worried about her. She kept almost passing out, so they figured they'd better sneak her home.

Didn't work. An adult bat has nothing on Jenny's mother's radar.

The next morning, Jenny's world was blackened by a behemoth headache. Her moans were like wind through

a monster cave. "I'll never drink anything again," she told her parents. "I swear."

Now, I'm pretty sure that Jenny will never become an alcoholic, but I'll say this about her promise: I don't believe it for a minute.

Not that I doubt her sincerity—that morning, even the faintest scent of vodka would have sent her straight back to the bathroom. She meant what she said.

But I still don't believe her. Call me a pessimist, if you will, but I'd have to see it to believe it. She'll never drink anything again? Doubtful. Very doubtful.

The book of the covenant ends with a few more "thou shalt nots," followed by a whole flurry of promises: "I'll send your enemies into chaos; I'll give you a piece of land that's absolutely wonderful; I'll rout anybody who stands in your way." Those are God's promises.

On one condition: that the people obey the laws God has given them.

"Hey, what a deal," the Israelites might have said. "You got it. Where do you want me to sign? Got a Bic handy?"

"All you have to do is obey," God says, "and I'll turn your deserts into paradise."

That's the deal. That's the whole package. It sounds so simple.

Excavations in the Middle East have shown that the Israelites actually did demolish a whole lot of sacred stones other nations worshiped. They listened—for a time.

But later, they forgot their part of the deal. Maybe their disobedience was less a matter of thumbing their noses at God's law than plain and simple forgetfulness. It doesn't really matter, though—ignorance is no excuse.

Would we do any better? If the Lord God Almighty spelled out for us exactly how we should live, then offered us the moon, the Brooklyn Bridge, and an uninhabited South Sea island, would we be any different? (That's exactly what God *has* done, of course.)

You may say yes. I say no. Obedience isn't something that comes naturally to us. In the end, breaking promises, like New Year's resolutions, is much easier. Ask Native Americans about broken promises. Ask the Israelites. Better yet, ask yourself.

I don't care if Jenny has a titanic hangover, I'm not betting on her promise. My doubts have less to do with her than with us. We simply don't have a great track record on promises—not on our own.

....

Even our most deeply-felt promises get broken,
Lord. In a world in which marriages fail so easily,
our word seems weak and sometimes meaningless.
Your word is not. Your Word is a light along
the paths of our lives. Thank you for meaning
what you say. Amen.

QUILTS

....

Read Exodus 24:1-11

Let's face it. I wouldn't be writing this—and you wouldn't be reading it—if the Bible were nothing more than a history text. It's God's Word. That's why we read it.

When I was a kid, I used to picture how the Bible was written in a specific way. I thought of God as a kind of chief executive officer, dictating to a secretary (in this case, Moses) exactly what to write. As God spoke, Moses wrote. Everything came out clear and smooth, like a seamless garment.

But that's not exactly accurate. Actually, Moses wasn't a secretary, and God didn't simply dictate while Moses sat on a halfway comfortable mountaintop rock.

In the passage for today, you can see some seams. Verses 1 and 2 should probably be glued on to verses 9 through 11: God calls Moses, Aaron, and some others to come up on the mountain (v. 1), and they do (vv. 9-11). It doesn't take some bearded old scholar to see that verses 3 through 8 interrupt a story that's already in progress. See what I mean?—there seem to be a few seams (sorry!).

Nobody knows exactly how the Bible got into its final shape, but a chapter like this one makes it likely the Bible is more of a scrapbook, really, than a dictated letter; a compilation of events and memories— here a piece, there a piece—that eventually tells the whole story of God and the people of God.

Let's just hang with the seam business here for a minute. You know, quilts are really popular again today, probably for a lot of reasons. Quilts, as you might know, are thick, warm blankets that women (usually) used to sew together from scraps of clothing and woven material, often forming beautiful patterns. A way of making beauty from very little, quilts have become great examples of folk art.

All over North America, people still make quilts, but it's the old quilts—the ones stitched together by women in "ye olden days"—that draw the crowds at shows.

Some of the most interesting old quilts tell the stories of peoples' lives—a bit of cloth from a wedding dress, some remnant of a child's play clothes, a scrap from a suit coat worn for a high school graduation. Years ago, when a woman made a quilt, she used cast-off material or remnants of fabric; so each part of the quilt was, in itself, a memory of some kind.

But even more, quilts had, and still have, their own kind of beauty. Each piece of cloth has value in itself, but when the whole quilt is finished it also becomes part of a new pattern. That means even if you don't know the history of each individual scrap, you can still enjoy the whole quilt's beauty.

Now, the Bible isn't a quilt. But when you get to passages like this one—where things are slightly out of order—it's helpful to remember that the whole passage, despite its patchwork quality, still has its own beauty.

What story does today's passage tell? That the covenant—God's promises and expectations of Israel—has been signed, sealed, and delivered. No matter how you read this passage, this truth comes through, loud and clear—Moses and the Israelites have signed on to be God's people.

And that—like a really great quilt—makes a beautiful story.

When we see the way things work together in the account of redemption, Lord, we're really amazed at how beautiful the whole story is. And, what's even better, we're part of it ourselves. The story of how you deal with your people is really our story as well because we are your people. In the name of your Son, Amen.

SIMPLY AWESOME

....

Read Exodus 24:12-18

I didn't plan on sitting in front of my computer this morning, but it rained last night and made the fields too muddy to walk. My kids and I had planned to be out in some Minnesota hayfield, helping a farmer pick up scads of trash.

That farmer needs help because his fields look like a tornado just whipped through. And they look that way because one did. Just forty-eight hours ago, fifty tornadoes spun out of a monstrous storm, terrorizing farms and small towns from eastern South Dakota to southwestern Minnesota, then making more trash in Illinois and Michigan.

Trash—that's about all that's left of a good hunk of a small town named Chandler, Minnesota. Someday, some Chandler families may read what I'm writing and start swapping stories—like the one about the metal stepladder a farmer found wrapped around a cow, or the house where people found their furniture rearranged in different rooms, or the big Honda hanging from a tree.

They won't tell stories about deaths in that storm, however, because there weren't any. The town's newly-repaired siren blasted just before the monster storm twirled out its venom. The people of Chandler had two minutes to hide. No one died.

Eric Prins, seventeen, ran away from the grain elevator where he was working and hid across the street in the bank vault. After the storm passed, he went to his home a few blocks away. But there was no home. He helped dig his mom and his sister Dana out of the mess.

Al Vis saw it coming and tried to outrun it in his car, but the power of this twister was so immense that, floored, the car couldn't go any faster than twenty-five miles per hour.

Jacoba Prinsen, seventy-one, headed downstairs to the basement, where she hid under a formica table. Later, digging through the rubble, she said, "If I wouldn't have been under that table, I wouldn't be here."

The huge black wall of wind scattered lumber around town like wooden matches. It picked up Dave De Jong's car from the road and buried it in mud a quarter-mile away. It sucked Dave's wife, Cindy, right out of the car, even though she had her seat belt on. Rescuers took one and a half hours to slice through the car and wrestle Dave and his eighteen-month old child out. It looks like they'll all be okay.

Betty Kooiman heard a rumbling and headed for the basement with Jonathan, her ten-year-old son. "It got stronger and stronger. I could hear glass flying, and I knew the house was going. It's a sound I will never forget."

When the Lord God took a seat on the mountain to dictate the law to Moses, the Israelites trembled. "The glory of the Lord looked like a consuming fire," the Bible says. You can imagine how the people cowered.

I've never been in a war, but it seems to me that very little else can come as close to stopping the human heart with fear than a tornado, an earthquake, or a typhoon—what some call "natural phenomena."

Already at eleven o'clock on the morning of Tuesday, June 16, the National Weather Service issued a severe weather warning to the areas that would be affected by the storm. It wasn't as if the tornadoes just came out of nowhere. Scientists know very well how tornadoes form.

Big deal. In spite of the warning, the people in Chandler felt totally powerless in the face of this frightful wind from the wide and swirling prairie sky. So you can imagine how shaken the Israelites must have felt in the face of God's consuming fire on the mountain.

That kind of power is incredible. Just incredible. Ask the folks from Chandler.

We stand or stoop in fear at the power of natural forces like hurricanes or earthquakes or tornadoes. We know that our best buildings don't stand a chance in the face of nature's power. Thank you for the assurance that you are stronger than storms. Thank you for signs of your power all around us. Amen.

THE WILL

....

Read Exodus 25:1-8

At the very end of Frederick Manfred's *Green Earth,* a long novel about the area of the country in which I live, Free Alfredson, the young man who feels himself departing from his parents' way of life, goes into his mother's bedroom for one last time. Throughout the novel, his mother's Christianity is treated respectfully; she's as devout as John the Baptist. But what she tells her son on her deathbed shocks him.

"I would very much like you in heaven with me someday," she says. "At the same time, though, I don't want you to pretend to be a Christian just to please me when privately you're not. Don't pose. Don't be a hypocrite . . . . Awful as the thought is, I think I'd much rather have you in hell, an honest soul, than in heaven, a hypocrite."

I don't care much for Mom Alfredson's theology—I'm not sure there'll be any hypocrites in heaven—but I understand what she feels very well. And, according to the passage you've read today, I think God understands it too.

We're about to begin six long chapters of really specific detail concerning the Lord's plans for the tabernacle, the place God will live while the Israelites are on the road. But before starting to list those specs, God says something we can't skip over easily.

It's about the gifts the people must bring as an offering in order to begin the tabernacle's construction. Those gifts, God says, should come only from certain people. "You are to receive the offering for me from each man whose heart prompts him to give."

I think God wants to be feared by us, all right. But that doesn't mean we should be like zombies, the living dead, kicking in funds just because we're scared to death of getting nailed—either by God or by other people. We're to be respectful of God's power, not simply to respond like trained monkeys to commands.

According to this passage, God is not interested in our gifts if the only reason we give them is fear; or if we give them just because we're *supposed* to. God wants the gifts we offer by our will, our choice.

It's that simple. The Lord wants the gifts of those who sincerely desire to give their firstfruits. Like Mrs. Alfredson, who wants her son to be honest, God wants only that which is willingly given.

Cain and Abel both brought offerings to God. Cain brought carrots, maybe peas and potatoes. Abel brought what the Bible calls "fat portions" from some of the firstborn of his flock.

People out here in hog and beef country could take that wrong and assume that God dislikes vegetarians, but we all know that's not the point. The very first murderer, Cain, brought an offering to the Lord—and who knows, maybe his carrots were the sweetest in town.

But, unlike Abel, he didn't bring that offering with a willing heart. And that's why the Bible says, "The Lord looked with favor on Abel and his offering, but on Cain and his offering he did not look with favor." Ouch! That's the kind of favor you don't want to be without.

Both brought offerings, but only Abel offered God his will.

God doesn't lock us into straightjackets. But the Bible tells us what the Lord has done, and it's clear God wants our appreciation. Our God wants to be wanted.

Mrs. Alfredson may have been wrong about hypocrites in heaven, but she was certainly in good company disliking hypocrites. Nobody loves 'em—not even the Lord.

"Only that person whose heart prompts him or her to give. That's all. I don't even *need* that," God could have said. "It's what I want."

Dear God, we know that sometimes we do things only because they're expected of us—not because we want to. Help us to shape our will toward thanksgiving. Give us joy in our salvation so that we will desire to bring our firstfruits to you. Amen.

THE ARK

....

Read Exodus 25:10-22

Whatever the ark was, today it's history. It would be great to travel to Israel and see this ceremonial relic, but it's long gone.

From the description in today's passage, we can only guess what it looked like. The NIV says the ark was a kind of chest, but even its exact size could start a fistfight at a convention of Bible scholars. What was a cubit, pray tell? Probably the length of a forearm, from tip to elbow. But no one really knows.

Some people think of the ark as a kind of throne. So if you want to draw a picture in your mind, you can envision a kind of carryable chest—on four legs—that resembles, in some way, a throne.

It would be great to buy a picture postcard of the ark, but of course, we can't. Even way back then, hardly anyone ever saw it. We know that later on, as King David performed a wild ceremonial dance, he had it brought to Jerusalem. We also know that Solomon put it in his temple, in the Most Holy Place. But we don't know a whole lot more about it.

And yet, the ark was the greatest of the Israelites' possessions. The ark! Remember the strange story of Uzzah (2 Sam. 6), who reached out to steady the ark when the oxen pulling it suddenly stumbled? Instant death. "The Lord's anger burned against Uzzah because of his irreverent act; therefore God struck him down" (v. 7). So the ark was never just some old museum piece.

We do know that the ark was decked out in the finest materials— pure gold, after all, isn't just any gold; it's gold cleaned up of all its impurities—impurities like silver, for instance.

It had an "atonement cover" (v. 17) of pure gold, probably a sheet-like covering on which the blood of sacrifice could be spilled. Sacrifice was necessary, of course. For God to be reconciled to the wandering people of Israel, there had to be some kind of sacrifice placed ceremoniously on the atonement cover.

You see, one of the miraculous features of God—both then and now—is the fact that God doesn't mock us by constantly saying, "I told you so," then leave us to live with the mess we make of our lives. He gives us a chance to reconcile ourselves to him, to bring ourselves back to his way of thinking.

For example, in the chapters we've looked at since the people of Israel left Egypt, God's code has been spelled out, and then the people have been asked to sign on the bottom line. "You keep my laws, and I'll bring you into the promised land. You've got dreams? I'll bring them to you in living color. Just be my people." "Sure," the Israelites say. "Where do we sign?" Promises, promises.

We make the same ones. But the fact is, we break those promises. And we need to make atonement, just like the Israelites of long ago.

Now, God could just laugh us off—simply turn from our antics forever. But here's the miracle in the Holy of Holies. God takes us back! Over and over again, God accepts our offerings of repentance. And that was the reason for the atonement cover.

"You'd better make a place for it, Moses," God likely told his servant. "And make it of purest gold. Because it's an important part of how I'm going to operate."

"Long after this ark has passed into foggy history, some blood will be shed—some very, very precious blood. So make this atonement cover pure—make it pure gold."

Our promises are as flimsy as the paper on which we write New Year's resolutions. But your promises never fail. You've provided the sacrifice for our sin, and for that we are grateful forever. May our lives sing your praise. Amen.

SOMETHING BORROWED

....

Read Exodus 25:23-40

Hammurabi, king of Babylon, was an important guy for a lot of rea-sons. But probably his greatest contribution to world civilization was a system of laws known by his name—the Code of Hammurabi.

The code has been considered by some to be the very first really important legal system in early civilizations. I'll let the historians argue about whether or not that's true.

In any case, Hammurabi's code influenced dozens of cultures in Mesopotamia and throughout the world. It established maximum prices for goods and services, and even determined a minimum wage. What Hammurabi accomplished for Babylon, Congress gets headaches trying to do for the United States: to set up a fair, flexible, and efficient system of taxes.

His code covered all kinds of areas: false accusations, military ser-vice, land and business regulations, family laws, tariffs, wages, trade, loans and debts, even witchcraft.

Historians agree that the foundation of Hammurabi's code is this principle: the strong in society should not come down hard on the weak. Thus, the code was based on the kind of justice we talk about—justice that respects the individual.

Some people claim that the laws we've already read through in the book of Exodus, as well as others contained in the Old Testament, bear a rather uncanny resemblance to the Code of Hammurabi. There are, in fact, lots of parallels. The really tough question is this—did the Israelites really receive all their laws from God's own hand, or did they, in fact, borrow a little from Hammurabi?

And as long as we're on to borrowing stuff here, let's push this prob-lem a little farther.

God's tabernacle—whose design and construction we're now going over—is long gone, of course. But most scholars agree that if we want to see something similar, we can look at another tabernacle, the Shrine of Tutankhamen. And guess what kind of ethnic background old Tut claimed? That's right, Egyptian. More than a little ironic, isn't it?

God's tabernacle has similarities to Egyptian shrines? The laws of the covenant have cousins in Hammurabi's code? How can that be? Didn't these things come directly from God?

And how about this? The "bread of the Presence" mentioned in today's reading is another kind of mystery. Who ate it? Some scholars claim that the idea of providing bread for the Lord in the temple was something the Israelites picked up from other religions—religions in which gods, like everyone else, needed to eat.

Now, if we aren't careful here, we can lose our belief that the Bible is the Word of God. If it's true that the Israelites just swiped all of their smarts, what part, really, did the Lord even play in the whole story?

Don't ever forget what's at the heart of the whole covenant, something we've already been over. God says that Israel, a nation of priests, is no island. And God's claim in Exodus 19, "The whole earth is mine," is no less true today than it was then.

God's hand doesn't just stir soup for the Israelites; the Creator prepares meals for all of creation. As the author of everything—even the Code of Hammurabi—God can borrow recipes without once plagiarizing.

After all, God made it all. God rules.

....

Don't let us get a big head about being your people, Lord. We know that the whole world is yours— you made it and it's in your control. Help us all to be your ministers in everything we do. Amen.

GOD'S DWELLING PLACE

....

Read Exodus 26

When I was a kid way back in the outrageous Sixties (only the Sixties decade gets its own capital letter), a lot of us thought we could change the world. And in some ways, we did. When thousands of us took to the streets, we changed the course of the nation. We stopped a war and made our society take another look at the way it was taking care of its poor and its minorities. For the most part, we questioned everything.

Some of us who wanted to change the world took jobs in the roughest parts of town. Those idealistic young kids figured that if they'd lend a hand to dealing with America's toughest problems—as social workers or teachers or whatever—maybe the whole mess our society was in would somehow straighten out. That's idealism.

What we were doing, of course, was following President Kennedy's famous line: "Ask not what your country can do for you; ask what you can do for your country."

All well and good. I think it's wonderful for young people to think they can change the world. After all, the Bible says somewhere that young folks shall see visions, doesn't it? Nothing wrong with a little idealism. Kids today could use some.

So, some of us took to the streets.

Now, working in some of the nation's toughest areas—the places where drive-by shootings happen weekly—is no piece of cake. But living there—especially if you're white—is, well, another thing altogether.

I remember a time when the residents of this country's inner cities got good and fed up with do-good white kids (and adults) who'd drive in from homes parked sweetly along the edges of country clubs and then try to tell those inner-city residents how to live. "If you want to have any credibility at all," they said, shaking their fists, "come here and live with us. Come right here and build a home."

That criticism makes sense. Real commitment, after all—deep commitment—means living in a neighborhood, not flying home at night to the safety of the suburbs.

The tabernacle, whose dimensions we've been looking at day by day, was God's address. If an Israelite were to ask, "Where can I reach the Lord?", the priest might well have answered, "Right there. See the tabernacle? You can find God right there."

It was God's own choice to dwell with the Israelites throughout their desert wanderings, and, at least at the beginning, in their new home in the promised land. And that dwelling place was the tabernacle itself, with all its tight specifications and plush furnishings. Its acacia wood frames, its curtains of finely twisted linen and its curtain of goats' hair, its fifty gold clasps, its gold rings on the crossbars—all of it was the place God called home.

By its very presence, this tabernacle and all its facilities told the Israelites that God wasn't off vacationing on the Riviera. Its message was perfectly clear: "I am here. I am living in your streets. I am with you. I am your God."

Thank you for living in us, Lord. Thank you for always being here, not somewhere else. Thank you for making us your temples. Amen.

HOME FREE

....

Read Exodus 27

You know, it's a shame there are places where kids can't play back-yard games. When I was a kid we just loved "Cut the Pie."

Somebody had to be "it," of course. Being "it" meant you had to face this maple tree that grew in our backyard and put your hands up over your head, while one of the other kids drew a circle—the pie—on your back. Someone else cut the pie—slashed a finger through it.

Then the kid who was "it" had to turn around and guess who the slasher was. If the kid was right, the slasher became "it"; if the kid was wrong, he or she was still "it."

But the it-kid got a punishment, too. Nobody wanted to stand around forever, so the punishment wasn't too horrifying. Usually it was something like this: "Count to fifty, kiss the picket fence, and bark three times like a chihuahua with a migraine."

After the punishment, "it" would set out on a hunt, wandering stealthily away from the maple, the place we called "gooooool" (I have no idea how to spell that word) to see if he or she could find any of the other kids peeking around corners. Kind of like "Hide and Seek."

If "it" would see someone, that kid would take off for the tree—gooooool—and at that point the game be-came a footrace. First one to gooooool wins—If "it" won, she'd say "One-two-three on Garibaldi" or whoever "it" was racing. But if the other kid got there first, he or she'd yell "home free."

Maybe you had to be there. It sounds kind of boring when I write it out.

Anyway, night after night we'd gather in our backyard and play "Cut the Pie." We thought it was great stuff. Okay, maybe it doesn't rank with Nintendo, but we played every night until well after dark.

What I remember best was how good it felt to scream "home free" at the top of my lungs. As long as I was touching the tree, you see, I wasn't "it." I was safe.

The altar of burnt offering, described in today's passage, stood in the courtyard of the tabernacle. It was the place where people brought their sacrifices, the place where blood was spilled and meat was burned.

The altar had horns of bronze on each corner. When animals were sacrificed, their blood was sprinkled on those horns as a kind of testament to the fact that a real sacrifice was made.

But here's the great part. If somebody got into trouble, that person could high-tail it for the tabernacle. And if he or she could reach the ark of burnt offering and grab hold of one of those horns, that person was home free, no matter who was in pursuit. You see, the horns were a real gooooool.

I'm serious. It's true. Read 1 Kings 1:50 for an example.

Imagine your life as someone who's been wrongly accused—nowhere to hide, nowhere to rest, no place to be "home free." You can't trust anybody, really, not as long as there's a bounty on your head. You're constantly looking over your shoulder, and your heart's always racing, your palms itchy.

But for the Israelites, the horns of the altar of burnt offering were a refuge, a place they couldn't be touched. Why? Because the horns themselves were bloody with the sacrifice made to God.

Imagine what life would be like without God, without a gooooool. But breathe easy. After all, in Christ, we're home free. All we need to do is to grab on to his sacrifice. Bing, bing, bing!

....

We know that in the middle of the worst pain, the greatest sorrow, the saddest loss—in the moments when we have no one else to turn to—you will be there, Lord, as you have been there for your people for thousands of years. You are our God. Thank you for making us part of your family. Amen.

ELEAZAR'S STORY

Read Exodus 28:1-28; Leviticus 9 and 10:1-3

It was a privilege granted to us, the nephews of Moses and sons of Aaron. We were chosen to be priests, specially appointed to watch over the sanctuaries, to offer sacrifices, to teach, and to minister to the people in the name of our God. To these tasks we were called.

Our being chosen was a blessed honor that none of us had earned. My brothers Nadab and Abihu felt the same way.

The day we heard what our tasks would be was a day I will never forget. Moses came to us and told us about everything—the garments we would wear, the ephod and the breastpiece—it was all so exact that we were speechless—all of us, even my father, Aaron.

I remember how my father nodded to his brother. We sat in Moses' presence that day—the four of us, our father, Aaron, in front of my brothers and me as Moses went over each detail of our specific tasks.

"Priests," Moses said—and there was a fire in his eyes that I'd seen before, the same fire I'd seen in Egypt as he stood before the great Pharaoh and never flinched. When a man sees God, his eyes are not the same as the eyes of others. After Moses had finished speaking to us, his lips twisted up into a tight smile, because behind the confidence he'd gained from the Lord lay his determination that we had a destiny. He knew that we as a people were not lowly slaves wandering aimlessly, but chosen and blessed by God.

And neither will I forget the day our ceremonies began, because it all went just as Moses had said. With my father leading, we killed the bull calf for the sin offering and a ram for the burnt offering, just as the Lord had commanded, and we did it in the presence of all the people so that the Lord might be honored.

We brought the blood to our father, Aaron. And he dipped his fingers and rubbed the blood on the horns of the altar, then poured the rest out at the base, just as he had been told.

My father slaughtered the burnt offering, then the offering for the people. Each time we did it as the Lord had said, everything just the way the Lord had told us through Moses.

When it was over, my father raised his hands and, in the name of God, blessed all the people there in the sanctuary. Then my father and Moses went into the tent. When they came out, the glory of the Lord shone around them. God's glory appeared to all of us that day, all of the people there in the sanctuary.

I have never seen such joy. The people were mad with happiness.

My brothers Nadab and Abihu were happy too, full of happiness—it was such a great feeling to be there. They wanted even more joy, more excitement. So they took their lamps and lit them and added even more incense. After all, they said, God is with us.

But then, right there, fire emerged from the presence of the Lord and killed them. My own older brothers, chosen, like me, to be priests—sons of Aaron, nephews of Moses. My own brothers, dead.

Our Lord God demands obedience.

I was there the day Moses told us what we, God's priests, would do for the Lord most high. And I was there, too, when my brothers, in their excitement, forgot that the Lord demands obedience, now and forever.

I am Aaron's son, Eleazar, brother of Nadab and Abihu. I am a priest of God, and when I teach the people today, as is my calling, I will teach them obedience to God, our deliverer.

....

Some stories seem so unfair, Lord. Some we understand, but we simply don't like. Help us to know you and to love you through your Word made flesh, Jesus Christ, our Savior. Amen.

THE DEATH OF PRIESTS

....

Read Exodus 29

Sometimes I think it would be so great if the Lord's hand showed up in our lives once in awhile, the way it showed up in the lives of the Israelites.

Think of it this way. You're at an anti-abortion rally somewhere and a real shouting contest erupts. Suddenly, God jams big fat corks into the mouths of all your opponents. Great trick.

Or how about this? Mac, the schoolyard bully, bellies up to little Deanie Weenie and starts to rub his knuckles over the top of the kid's head. Not for any good reason, of course—he does it every day just to keep DW humble, he says. But this time God spots Mac picking on poor DW, and, in a wink, zaps him buck naked. Big Mac stands there in the raw, the whole school bellering with laughter.

Or this. Life is really rough for the Smithsons. They lost their house to a fire caused by lightning. Mr. Smithson had a job as an accountant before his company merged and the new honchos shut down the plant where he worked. Angela broke her leg when she got hit riding her bicycle to school. Then, all of a sudden, Mrs. Smithson developed cancer. Makes you want to cry. But then people start to pray. And just like that Mrs. Smithson's cancer hightails it. Dad gets hired on by a good company. And to top it off, a man they met at a campground in the Black Hills three years ago leaves them a half-million dollars, just because he considered the Smithsons such a fine Christian family.

Don't you sometimes just wish God would act that way?

I do. But then I read a passage like Leviticus 10, part of yesterday's reading. The passage describes how Aaron's sons Nadab and Abihu, during the week they were consecrated as priests (as outlined in today's passage), were suddenly, almost mysteriously, struck dead by fire raging from the sanctuary of God.

You see, the plans God gave Moses for the consecration of the priests, the plans you read about today, were eventually carried out. Everything worked just the way God said. Once the blood had been properly doused and the sacrifices accomplished, we're told that the people "shouted for joy" (Lev. 9:24).

Amid all this happiness, these two young guys took it upon themselves to add to the celebration. They lit their lamps once more, excited, perhaps, by the people's joy. Then, boom!—they were dead. Just like that.

Aaron remained silent, the Bible says. And when he did speak to his two remaining sons, he told them not to mourn for their brothers.

It's an incredible story. And it follows, with nearly exact detail, the prescriptions God established in today's passage.

You know, if God really were to enter our lives in the same way as God entered the Israelites' lives, I wonder how many church soloists—people who allow their excitement to overshadow their love and devotion to God—we'd see struck down?

For that matter, how about me? Here I sit, trying to turn a phrase just perfectly. How many times is it only the perfect-sounding phrase that I'm after when I write a sentence? How many times does my own pride get in the way of what God expects of me, God's servant?

I know the answer. A lot. There are no perfect priests, no one who gets all the commands right. No perfect scores in the big exam of our lives. We've all got egos. Nadab and I.

But through Christ, our bloody sacrifice, thank God, we're forgiven.

---

*Grant us the power to give all of our best to you,
Lord, in everything we do, every day. May our
lives be dedicated to thanks for your marvelous
gift of love. Amen.*

IS NOTHING SACRED?

....

Read Exodus 30

Not long ago, an organization called the NEA, the National Endowment for the Arts, got itself into big trouble because it paid artists to do work that some people considered to be really, really vile, even blasphemous.

You may remember the name Robert Mapplethorpe. Mapplethorpe was a photographer, a homosexual, who died of AIDS. Before he died, however, the NEA gave him a grant to do his photography. And after he died, an exhibition of his work toured the country. Some of his photographs were of naked men—but not just naked like Michelangelo's "David." Some of Mapplethorpe's naked men were photographed doing what lots of folks considered absolutely disgusting.

The NEA got in trouble for it. They also got in trouble for funding the work of a man who dunked a cross in a beaker of his urine and called it art. Loads of people were enraged that such "art" was paid for by the United States government.

They were right to be upset, I think. We live in a culture that prides itself on freedom of expression. If somebody wants to dunk a cross in urine, then in North America—whether we like it or not—he or she has that right. But people who think such "art" is disgusting should not have to pay for it.

The focus of today's entire chapter—the altar of incense, the atonement money, the basin for washing, the anointing oil—is on what God considers to be *sacred.* These things, the Lord says, are really special.

Sacred is a word we don't use very much. Sometimes people still refer to "sacred music," but other than that, can you remember the last time you heard anyone use the word *sacred* in any conversation? What's sacred?

People got really, really angry about that cross in the artist's urine because it was blasphemy—that is, it used something sacred contemptuously. People believe that the cross is something sacred.

But is any cross—just because it's shaped like one—really sacred?

What about the cross little Sammy pounds into the soft earth over the grave of his pet rabbit? He nails together two old plaster laths, sharpens one end, and sticks it in the ground. Is that cross sacred?

Here's another example. I used to mow the grass at the state park where I worked. Just a little way from the campground was a place in the trees where people could worship—logs for benches and up front a cross, this one of white birch lashed with twine. I mowed the grass around it, but I don't remember feeling as if that birch cross was some- how sacred.

You know, you're accustomed to getting answers from me in these little meditations, but this time I'm not giving any.

I'm wondering—maybe you're wondering too—is there really any- thing sacred in our lives? Some Christian religions, of course, have all kinds of sacred objects—shrouds, images, even chunks of what is supposed to be part of the original cross.

I really can't think of anything—any object—that is truly sacred. Can you? Even my expensive study Bible is all marked up.

Today you read an entire chapter in which God vividly instructs Moses to make certain objects absolutely sacred, untouchable, be- cause those objects have been touched by God.

If you can think of something really sacred, write me. Maybe we're missing something here. Maybe we need something sacred.

....

The story of Aaron's son shows us clearly that your
word is sacred. Not the Bible itself, of course, but the
truth of your love for us. Help us never to violate
what is sacred—your offering of love.
In Jesus' name, Amen.

BEZALEL AND THE REFORMATION

....

Read Exodus 31:1-11

All the way through the book of Exodus, Moses has been the star. It was Moses, after all, who dropped his shoes at the burning bush, Moses who was given all the instructions on how to deal with Pharaoh, Moses who raised his arms at the Red Sea, and Moses who snuck up closest to the Lord God Almighty on Mount Sinai. No wonder Charlton Heston wanted the part of Moses in the blockbuster *The Ten Commandments.*

For the most part, Moses has been in the lead because he was the middle man, the mediator, the one human being chosen by God to tell everything to the Israelites. How many times haven't we read an introductory clause like the one that opens today's passage, "Then the Lord said to Moses"?

The Bible never says, "Then the Lord said to Aaron," or Miriam, or anybody else. All the way through it's been Moses who runs in the plays God calls from the sidelines—I mean, the mountain.

And that's important. Bing, bing, bing! The only one real mediator between God and humankind is the Son of God, the one we've sometimes referred to as the Bread-Man, Jesus Christ. All these passages we've been reading illustrate the fact that God's people need a mediator (a Moses, or a Christ) to bring in the plays—in order to know which plays to run (I'm still on football here).

But today's passage is different. In this chapter, God seems to have simply bypassed his one-and-only. He says, in the past tense, "I have *chosen* Bezalel, son of Uri, the son of Hur, of the tribe of Judah, and I have filled him with the Spirit of God." It's a done deal. This is news to Moses, who suddenly feels a kind of end-around going right past him.

If Moses had an ego, he could have been miffed here. God not only chose to communicate this time without using Moses as a go-between, but God also specially chose someone other than Moses to do the artwork for the tabernacle. After conveying all God's specific requirements about this, that, and the other piece of tabernacle tapestry to the people, Moses might have had the urge to sit down himself and pound brass into something God-worshiping beautiful.

But if Moses did feel miffed, we don't read it, of course. And it's quite likely he didn't feel slighted anyway. You can bet he had enough irons in the fire already. Maybe he was happy to leave the artwork up to Bezalel.

I like this passage, though, not only because I like art—writing is an art, after all—but because I think it's the first hint of the Protestant Reformation.

You see, the Reformation of the church several hundred years ago rode along on Luther's brainstorm that salvation comes by faith, not by some church decree. At least one of the primary ideas of the Reformation is that we are, therefore, all priests; no single human being stands between God's promises and our lives. That means that each one of us (I'm going to use the word here) is *sacred*, not just some of us who have a certain kind of education and get to baptize kids. All of God's people who offer their lives—their living—to God are God's priests.

God came to Bezalel and Oholiab because they had talents, gifts—they were artists. And this time God didn't go through Moses. He went right into the artist's studio and said, "I like your work, Bezalel. I want it."

God says the same to all of us. Isn't that great?

....

It is such a joy for us to think that our studying and our singing and our housekeeping and our carpentry and our fields of corn and clover can sing your praise, Lord. It's such a blessing to think we can serve you in all that we do. Thank you for the privilege of bringing glory to your name. Amen.

GROUPTHINK

....

Exodus 32:1-6

Right now, in Sioux Center, Iowa, I'm a sucker for men's earrings.

A few nights ago, a neighbor kid came over, and I noticed right away he had an earring. Nôw some of you live in places where lots of guys wear earrings or where only a certain kind of guy wears an earring. But in the high school my daughter attends, a guy with an earring would probably draw as many eyes as a girl who whacked off her hair.

I've got to admit it—I liked it. "Hey, André," I said, "great earring." Actually, it was so tiny it was hardly visible.

He looked a little sheepish, and then said he was wearing it only because his parents were away on vacation. "It's fake," he said.

Too bad.

It may well be that I'm a sucker for men's earrings because I grew up in a time when some kids wore outlandish stuff just to show they weren't cut from the same mold as everybody else. And I know very well that it's possible for earrings—just like long hair or billowy bellbottom jeans—to become a fad, something everybody wears, oddly enough, not to be out, but in.

But right now, in Sioux Center, Iowa, guys' earrings are not a fad, and that's why I liked this little gold band clipped to André's ear.

I told you before, I've been reading about Hitler. No single story in the whole twentieth century is so horrifying. What Hitler did in Germany was to mold a single mind from a whole nation. He liked to say that he designed the Volkswagen, the look-alike car for all kinds of look-alike people.

Hitler would have hated guys with earrings, and what's worse, he would have convinced everybody else to hate them too. If you've ever seen movies of Hitler shouting at thousands of people, flags waving all over, the people holding their arms aloft and screaming, "Heil, Hitler," you've seen the greatest twentieth-century example of "groupthink." People willingly tossed their own individual minds into Hitler's poison soup.

Hitler sweet-talked an entire nation into believing that getting rid of millions of innocent people was really a good thing. Talk about a lie. And the horror is not only that millions of people died, but that other millions of people actually believed the poison sweet talk.

I liked André's earring because, in a silly way maybe, it said something about André: "I've got my own mind."

The story of the golden calf is another horrifying story of groupthink so strong that even Aaron, brother of Moses, staring at thousands of worked-up Israelites, didn't dare stand up for what was right. He just couldn't look in the face of all that pressure and say, "Folks, you're wrong. Now settle down. Go home and watch TV."

It's a whole lot easier to get on the bandwagon. "Okay, okay," Aaron says, "cool it. We'll make an idol." The crowd throws up their arms!

Individualism, putting yourself before others, can be sinful. But there's nothing righteous about groupthink, or tagging along with the crowd just to stay part of it. The real test of character, as we've seen before in Exodus, is obedience. With Moses on the mountain for forty long days and nights, the Israelites' will buckled like a bad knee.

André's parents are back again, so right now that little earring is probably hidden in his drawer. Too bad, because right now, in Sioux Center, Iowa, I guess I'm a sucker for earrings.

Give us strength, Lord, to stand up against whatever it is that keeps us from obedience. Thank you for Moses' example of standing in for his people. In Jesus' name, Amen.

QUIZ TIME

....

Read Exodus 32:7-14

You know, the slower you read the Bible, the more interesting it is. Take a story like this one about the golden calf. It sticks with you. It's not a sweet story, but wow!—is it memorable. Read it closely, and it's even harder to shake.

Moses is up on the mountain, scribbling down laws, when suddenly the Lord interrupts the dictation. "Say, Moses," God says, "I'm starting to boil because *your* people—the ones *you* brought out of Egypt—are making me mad down there in the foothills. You'd better get down there."

It sounds, actually, a lot like something I might say to my wife. If one of our kids is acting less than angelically, I'm likely to say, "Barbara, you better speak to your daughter (or son)."

My wife is no dummy. She knows when I say *"your* daughter" I'm trying to shake off responsibility for whatever bad stuff *my* daughter did.

And here's the fascinating thing. Moses knows what God means when he uses *your* that same way. Look at how Moses responds (v. 11): "Why should your anger burn against *your* people, whom *you* brought out of Egypt?" he asks. Moses uses the same trick of speech that God used.

Family members often develop their own little tricks of speech—words like cue cards that don't translate easily outside the family. Obviously, Moses and the Lord have developed their own way of communicating. You see, to God, Moses is family. Moses has a really special relationship with the Creator of the world.

In the rest of the passage, that relationship goes through a test of sorts, a quick quiz.

The book of Exodus records over and over a promise the Lord makes to Moses—that the Israelites can depend on God's love always. Now the people are giving God a reason to drop that promise. In little more than a month, those same people that God has promised to love are flat on their faces before a statue with gold for brains. God certainly has a right to get mad.

And for a minute, the Lord really seems to lose it. God offers Moses a deal he can't refuse—"Hey," says God, "phooey on them. I'll make *you* the great nation, Moses."

Moses isn't interested in fame, though; he's interested in God staying God. Right now, as Moses sees it, the Lord almost seems to have forgotten those promises to love Israel. Instead, God seems ready to torch the whole mess at the foot of the mountain.

Moses holds God back from carrying out that threat—or does he? I wonder.

The truth is, I think, Moses simply passes a test here. Not only does he turn down the cushy offer of wealth and power, the chance to become the new Abraham, he also begs God to cool down and remember all those earlier promises to the Israelites. "What's really at stake here," Moses says, "is you—your good name. After all, you back out now and the Egyptians sing 'I told you so' for years."

And with that, the Bible says, God appears to cool off.

I think God was bluffing. I think it was a test to see how Moses would react. Moses aces the quiz because he knows God's love is so much greater than ours that it's not even in the same league. He knows God loves us *in spite of* the long, lonesome trail of our broken promises.

Moses passes the quiz because he knows God. He's part of God's family. So are we. But the Lord isn't just "Dad" either—the Lord is our God. And God always means what God says.

The Israelites, on the other hand, weren't particularly good at meaning what they said. But then, they aren't alone, I guess, are they?

*Thank you for heroes like Moses, Lord. Thank you
for their testimony in your Word. May the
importance of the story of your redemption grow
in our hearts. Amen.*

THINGS ARE NOT WHAT THEY SEEM

....

Read Exodus 32:15-24

Driving Miss Daisy won four Academy Awards, but it will never spawn a sequel. The movie had no mind-bending special effects, no vampires, aliens, or terminators. In my book, though, *Driving Miss Daisy* makes any *Batman* movie you want to nominate look like over-hyped comics. (Okay, my son disagrees, but he's not writing this book.)

I loved *Miss Daisy*. It had cars, but no chases; love, but no bed scenes. It's about race, but only prejudice gets hammered.

At the very end of the movie, Hoak, Miss Daisy's chauffeur, who's an old black man, comes to visit Miss Daisy at the rest home where she lives. All the way through the movie, the friendship between these two grows and grows, even though the differences between them—Miss Daisy, a rich white woman, and Hoak, a poor black man—span miles.

It's Thanksgiving Day, and even though Miss Daisy is lonely, she's not about to admit she's happy to see her old friend. When Hoak points at an untouched piece of pumpkin pie in front of her, Miss Daisy tries to pick up a fork. Physically, she can't, so Hoak does, and then feeds her that Thanksgiving pie, slowly and lovingly. Very little is said because actions, in movies and in life, often speak louder than words.

All right, I got tears in my eyes. I'll admit it.

The scene where Hoak helps Miss Daisy eat the pie is really a sym-bol, and before you decide to skip what I'm going to say because you always hated English class, let me say this: don't.

A symbol is something that means what it is—plus a whole lot more. Hoak helping Miss Daisy eat pumpkin pie is almost like a human com-munion. His slowly bringing the forkful to her lips is more than just eat-ing—it's love. A picture that says it all.

Today's passage contains two symbols. Neither of them are any-where as sweet as the one that puts a wrap on *Driving Miss Daisy*. But they're both as unforgettable as Hoak's forkful of pumpkin pie. They're both what they are—plus a whole lot more.

Moses comes down from the mountain in a rage and breaks the stone tablets God had inscribed. Few actions in the Bible are as memorable as that, not only because Moses' furnace boils over, but also because the tablets smashing all over the rock are a symbol of the promises the Israelites had broken, promises they'd signed for not more than a half-semester ago. Those smashed stone tablets are a picture of broken promises. They are what they are and a whole lot more.

But Moses wasn't through yet. One rampage wasn't enough. He pulverizes the golden calf, dumps its powder in the water, and makes the Israelites drink. Why? Scholars have more than one opinion on what Moses meant to do here, but at least one good reason for his actions is clear. Every last Israelite shared responsibility for what happened while Moses was away on Mount Sinai. The tainted water is another symbol. It's more than just water. It's their own sin.

And it's not just the story that makes this scene so memorable. What's the big deal about Moses blowing his cool all over the foothills? The big deal is this: things are what they seem, but they're a whole lot more, too. Broken tablets—broken promises—broken world in need of a Savior. Bing, bing, bing!

....

It seems to us almost incredible that the Israelites could
so quickly abandon their faith, Lord, and yet we know
that we sometimes do the same.
Forgive us our weakness and strengthen
us with your love. Amen.

SAVING FACE

....
Read Exodus 32:22-24

I can't help laughing at the lame excuse Aaron gives when Moses asks him what's been going on back at the home front. What Aaron says is so incredibly dumb. Even so, I have to admit there's an Aaron in me too.

Moses flings down the stone tablets, crushes the golden calf, makes the Israelites drink of their own sin, and then turns to his brother. (Remember, Aaron was an eyewitness to God's tremendous acts in Egypt; in fact, he had even played a role in those events.)

"Aaron," Moses says, "What did these people do to you to make you go along with their sin?"

(Moses assumed that the only way the Israelites could have pushed his brother into such incredible stupidness was by threatening him with a spatter of fishing hooks in the earlobe.)

But Aaron knows the temperature of the water he's in. Before he even starts to answer, he gets to the point. "Don't be angry," he says.

Fat chance. Aaron's already seen God's own stones smashed into smithereens. "Cool off," Aaron says.

And offers lie number one. Aaron claims the Israelites were so super-anxious about their leader, Moses, that they'd simply requested something to soothe their concern. "The people didn't know where you were," he tells Moses, his face as wrinkled as a washboard.

Cute. But Aaron's nose is about to extend to Macedonia because then comes lie number two. Aaron must figure that Moses is into miracles, so he dreams up a stupendous scenario of his own. "I told them to give up their gold jewelry," he tells Moses, "and I threw it into the fire." Now listen to this. "Just like that, bingo!—out came a golden calf."

Sure.

Moses doesn't even respond.

As lame excuses go, Aaron's is major-league.

But like I said, the whole scene would really be a kick if it weren't so human.

Ricky heads into Target and grabs a Nintendo game, sticks it in the big pocket of his jacket, and heads for the door.

The store detective sees him, grabs him by the shoulder (ouch!), and tells him to come to the back of the store. Checks his pocket, and sure enough—there's Dazzling Donkey, or whatever it was Ricky heisted.

"What do you call this?" the store detective says. He's smoking a little cigar, one of those with an off-white holder.

"I swear," Ricky says, "I was just holding it in my pocket and I must have forgotten to pay for it when I went through the checkout."

Sure. Cute. Really slick. Watch Ricky's nose. He's got nothing on Pinocchio. The store cop might die laughing if he didn't hear the same song and dance every day of his life.

Or, how about this one? Guy named Adam eats an apple he was told not to eat. God comes visiting the next afternoon. Adam hides, scared stiff, because of what he's done. God finds him. "Adam, where have you been?" God says. "I've been looking for you."

"I didn't want you to see me," Adam says. "I just didn't have a decent thing to wear."

Sure. Cute.

But we all do it. And saving face—or trying to—is always silly.

The thing is, only the Lord saves face. We don't save our own.

Thanks be to God, who loves us.

....

We all have made up stories to protect ourselves, Lord. When we see it in Aaron we recognize it because it's so familiar. Forgive us for protecting ourselves at all costs—at the cost, even, of sin. Thank you for your eternal mercy upon us. Amen.

CARNAGE

....

Read Exodus 32:25-29

In some places in the United States, death by violent crime occurs with such regularity that it has become as ordinary a part of life as graduating from high school or getting married. Since 1968, the number of murders and violent crimes in America's twenty largest cities has doubled, and there appears to be no end in sight.

Ninety percent of all violent crimes are committed by males, and males are also most often its victims. Murder has become the leading cause of death for young black males.

In the last year or so, most everyone in North America has seen two really awful videotapes. The events pictured in one of them, the police beating of Rodney King in Los Angeles, led to the events of the other—young black residents of south central Los Angeles assaulting Reginald Denny, a white truck driver who happened to be in the wrong place at the wrong time.

Those two tapes dramatize and even increase many of our basic fears—terrifying police brutality on inner-city blacks, and terrifying random violence on suburban whites who venture into the cities. No other Western nation suffers so much human violence.

How does the United States deal with crime? No other industrialized nation uses capital punishment as we do here in the States, because most other nations consider the death penalty—simply murdering murderers—to be barbaric and immoral.

Now, you may well be in favor of capital punishment—many North Americans favor it; many oppose it. But no one I know, not even the staunchest supporters of the death penalty, would argue that we ought to kill *all* criminals. Nobody. Even those most interested in cleaning up crime recognize that killing criminals is serious business. The death penalty should never be imposed without convincing evidence and real soul-searching.

Today's short passage makes it painfully clear that our world is not the world of the desert-wandering Israelites. The carnage that Moses commands of the Levites—the murder of three thousand golden calf worshipers—is something no Christian can read without wincing.

Moses tells the Levites to go and kill even those closest to them—family and friends and neighbors. It's horrible.

This story is difficult to read. Lots of questions remain. Earlier in the chapter, it seems that all of Israel had worshiped some kind of idol; yet, here, only three thousand (out of what was probably hundreds of thousands) are punished with death. Why? Are we to believe that Aaron danced to the tune of only a fraction of the people? The Bible doesn't explain.

How do we, as Christians, deal with horror stories like this one? Imagine the scene. Imagine the carnage. In tents and on dirt paths all around the camp, blood flows thickly and pools in the desert sand.

We know *why*, of course. The people were punished for their unbelief. Moses says the Israelites have become a laughingstock to the nations. The chosen people dropped their faith in God like a bad habit and went dancing after dummies. The crime, the sin, is clear, but—brothers and sisters murdered by Levite swords? It's awful to think about.

Sometimes, we don't understand everything. Sometimes, we simply bite our tongues, and wish really hard that we did understand. We know only that the God of Israel's incredible escape from Egypt demands obedience.

Sometimes the Lord says only this: "Be still and know that I am God."

Dear Lord, we can't help but be horrified by the death of so many Israelites. Your anger is hard for us to understand and bear. Help us to live in obedience, and thank you for sending your Son to take the burden of our sin away, leaving us safe beneath your hand. Amen.

GREATER LOVE HATH NO MAN OR WOMAN . . .

....

Read Exodus 32:30-35

You want to read a line that will pin your ears back? How about this: "When Christ calls a man, he bids him come and die."

You can spend a lot of time hanging around Christian people and never hear a line that makes you gulp quite so deeply.

That line came from Dietrich Bonhoeffer, a young German pastor who dared to oppose Hitler. For Bonhoeffer, opposing the Nazi mob on the basis of God's command to love was an invitation to die for Christ.

When Hitler rose to power in 1933, some members of the church in Germany began to support Hitler. At the same time, Bonhoeffer and some others broke away to form what came to be called the "Confessing Church."

Twice during those years, Bonhoeffer could have escaped the ugliness of Nazi Germany. Once, when he took a pastorate in London; and later, when he accepted an opportunity to study in America after being forbidden by the Nazis to speak publicly in Germany in 1939.

But escaping the evil mushrooming in his native land wasn't what Bonhoeffer wanted. He felt that anyone who ran away during the horror had no right to be a part of the rebuilding when Hitler was finally defeated. Twice he left, and twice went back into the fire.

Some people who hated Hitler learned to keep their mouths shut and lay low. Not Bonhoeffer. When he returned to Germany, he worked hard for the resistance. To the Nazis, he was a traitor. But there was no question for Bonhoeffer—his obedience was pledged not to the Führer, but to God.

Bonhoeffer paused when he learned of an attempt to assassinate Hitler, for even in this situation, he questioned murder. But finally he concluded that the Christian's obligation in Nazi Germany was more than to comfort the sorrowing; it was to end the suffering. Some Christians may well disagree with Bonhoeffer's opinion, but he stood firmly behind it.

The plot to kill Hitler failed. And, under torture, one of conspirators gave Bonhoeffer's name to the SS, Hitler's security forces. He was taken to Tegel prison, tortured and interrogated, then isolated in solitary confinement.

On April 5, 1945, the day Hitler decided that none of those who had conspired to kill him would live, Bonhoeffer was sent to a detention camp at Schonberg. On April 8, he began to preach a sermon in the prison. He was interrupted by guards, who ordered him to collect his things. Taken to Flossenburg concentration camp, Bonhoeffer was sentenced to death. He was hanged on April 9, 1945.

There was no funeral. There is no stone. Bonhoeffer's body was burned, his ashes flung to the wind. But his story is not forgotten. You're reading that story right now, perhaps for the first time.

People say that we have no heroes today, no men or women to look up to for plain and simple courage. But we have Bonhoeffer.

And we have Moses. Reading the terrible story of the golden calf, we suddenly stumble on the incredible heroism of the man who first heard the I AM at the burning bush. "If you can't forget the sin of your people," Moses says to God, "then blot me out of your book."

Now, that's a hero. Moses offers himself as a sacrifice for the sins of his people, God's people. "Let them alone," he says, "just take me."

God doesn't take him up on the offer. There will be punishment for those who are guilty, says the Lord. That will be taken care of later.

But, as we know, an even greater hero was still to come—a Savior, who would die for the sins of all the people. Jesus Christ did come, and died, for our sake.

....

When we read about the apostles—or martyrs like Bonhoeffer—it seems as if their lives are so different from our own that it's impossible to see ourselves in them. But, Lord, help us to surrender ourselves to you in the same way they did—heart, mind, body, and soul. Help us, in Jesus' name. Amen.

ANTHROPOMORPHISM

....

Read Exodus 33:1-3

Let this meditation serve as a warning to eighth-grade girls in Sioux Center, Iowa. A few nights ago Scotty Rynders (names have been changed here to protect the loony), said out loud, in the presence of our whole family, that someday he's going to want a wife who's strong enough to sit on him but good.

What a line!

Scotty thinks of himself as a lit fuse. Unless he's got someone around to douse the sparks, time and time again he's going to blow up.

Now I'm warning young women about this because it's my opinion—and I may be wrong—that most girls (and most guys, for that matter) wouldn't want to spend a lifetime as a fireman (or woman). Who'd want to grow old constantly jerking a steel bit through wild-man Scotty's choppers? That's no job for a dog, not even a pit bull.

I still laugh when I think of Scotty's confession. But I'll give him this much—if it's true, then at least he understands himself. If he is some kind of jungle beast in need of a thick leash, then at least he knows what he is. Socrates would have liked Scotty. After all, it was Socrates who claimed that the first rule of thumb for everyone is "know thyself." Scotty knows—or thinks he knows—he's untamed.

In fact, Scotty's self-appraisal isn't all that much different from God's self-appraisal in this chapter. The dust still hasn't settled completely on the golden calf incident and its aftermath, and now God is setting out some new guidelines for the Israelites' remaining trek through the desert.

"Things have changed," the Lord says to Moses. But the basic objective is the same: the people of Israel—God's chosen people—are still bound for the land promised to Abraham, Isaac, and Jacob. What's more, God is still going to deliver all of this land to them, despite the fact that the various "Ites" presently have their tents pitched on the promised land.

"But I will not go with you," God tells Moses. "There's been a change in plans here. You are a stiff-necked people, and I might destroy you on the way."

I don't think Scotty took his cue from this passage, but what he said about his needs in a wife isn't all that much different from the kind of confession God seems to be making here. God's worried that, in the presence of the Israelites, all previous promises might be forgotten in the face of an overwhelming urge to rub them out.

It's strange to think God Almighty might be concerned about a hair-trigger temper. It makes God seem more human than divine.

Of course, sometimes the Bible does that—makes God out to be almost human. That's called *anthropomorphism,* a big fat utility word that means ascribing human qualities (in this case, an out-of-control temper) to God. Making our God seem like us is a way we have of trying to understand what God is like.

But that's not the importance of today's passage. At the end of the previous passage, Moses placed himself right between God and the people as a mediator. Now the withdrawal of God's presence from the Israelites indicates that it's going to take another mediator to keep God from punishing those mumbling, grumbling people—and us.

Here's what's got to happen: Someone is going to have to go between God and humankind—that's the whole story. Bing, bing, bing!

....

When we see your anger at your people, Lord, we
wonder how you can choose to keep loving them—
and us. But you do. For keeping that promise
forever, we thank you, Lord. Amen.

LEFT BEHIND

....

Read Exodus 33:4-6

I was only eight years old the night we left Egypt. It was a night no one will ever forget, a terrible night of screaming and dying. My father stood before me; I remember he was very nervous.

We were spared, of course. Because my father had painted our doorstep with the blood of a lamb, as we had been instructed. All over Egypt, death came with the wind. But in my father's house there was no death.

That night, for the first time in my life, I felt important. We were slaves, you remember. My father worked in the house of Evita, a nobleman. And even though he didn't make bricks, as so many Hebrew fathers did, he suffered the way we all did when the Lord God of Abraham began to bring plagues down on the heads of the Egyptians.

I remember the candle lit in our home, and I remember seeing my father standing before me. I had fallen asleep. My father and mother were getting things ready because we were leaving, as we'd been told. My father said that finally the Egyptians would send us away, finally they'd do anything to escape the God of Israel.

In the candlelight, I remember seeing my father's hands full of jewelry.

"I don't want it," my mother said.

"Evita told me to get out," my father told her. "'What is it you want?' he said to me. 'Is it our gold?' Then he took it off his own neck, and off his children's necks, and shoved it into my hands."

"It's extra weight. It will remind me of the Egyptians," my mother said. "I don't want it. Leave it behind."

"We must take it," my father said. "We have been commanded to take their jewelry for an offering to God."

Then my mother opened her shawl in silence. That night of the Passover, my father left the Egyptian jewelry with her.

Later on, when we were wandering in the wilderness, I was often afraid of the Lord, but I was not afraid of my people. Except once— when Aaron made the golden calf. I was afraid because that day I

didn't know my own father. Something happened to him, something that I've never really understood.

"Give me the jewelry," he told my mother. "Aaron wants all our gold to make an idol." He stood over her, his eyes aflame. "No one can live on that burning mountain, Rachel," he said. "Look for yourself— Moses is gone. It's a new day. We need a god of gold."

My mother did not respond. My father stared at her angrily, and neither of them moved. I thought he would hit her, I really did. Then, finally, my father's eyes fell and he left the tent.

And after all the dying, he returned once again for the jewelry. Nothing was said between them. I was very young. He stood there once more over my mother, in silence. Three thousand people had died.

My mother placed the necklaces and armbands into my father's waistcloth, and, still in silence, he left the tent.

I followed him because I loved those armbands. At the foot of Mount Horeb, my father stood in the company of thousands of Hebrews, all of them in silence, and left the jewelry there in the thick dust and the burning heat of that desert mountain.

I saw him cry. It was not for the jewelry. I was young, but I had ears and eyes, and I knew why my father cried.

Something else, something far greater than Egyptian jewelry, was lost that day. I knew it too, even though I was very young.

....

Forgive us, Lord, when we decide that other things are more important in life than the blessings we've been given from your hand. Forgive our chasing after other gods. Thank you for always forgiving us in your Son's name. Amen.

CITY LIMITS

....

Read Exodus 33:7-11

Time out here for a little lesson in the way stories work.

Here's a plot: "When the King died, the queen died of grief." We call it a *plot* because its action—two deaths—is related: the queen dies of a broken heart *because* her loving hubby died before her. Plot is sequential action, like a falling row of dominoes.

Now, here's the same plot with something extra: "King Babbles died of hardening of the arteries when he was fifty-two, but then, he shouldn't have gorged so much fried pork. Queen Mop, whose father owned a Studebaker dealership in PagoPago, felt so bad that she pigged out herself on her husband's junk food. Woe and woe to Queen Mop."

I'm being silly, of course. But I am trying to make a point. Every story has plot, but it also has some extra stuff. That extra stuff is called *exposition.* When I teach kids how to write stories, I tell them that the extra stuff is almost always boring when compared to the plot, because plot is action and extra stuff, exposition, is only—yawn—explanation.

Exposition is essential to a story. But too much of it, and readers start nodding off.

We've arrived at what looks like a passage of extra stuff. You can tell it by looking at the verbs. "Now Moses *used to* take a tent and pitch it outside the camp some distance away, calling it the 'tent of meeting.'" *Used to* means he did it quite often, not just one day. *Used to* seems to indicate we're being told extra stuff here.

Even people who read a lot of stories are likely to let their minds wander at this point. After all, until now everything we've seen since Moses came down off the mountain has been straight plot—Moses sees the golden calf, so he smashes the stone tablets and makes the Israelites drink the dusty water. Then he commands the death of those guilty of forgetting the Lord, their deliverer. God gets angry, Moses is told God will no longer hang around the Israelites' tents, and Moses commands the Israelites to dump all their jewelry in the sand. First this, then that, then that. Plot.

Now, suddenly, we get extra stuff. "By the way, Moses used to go to this tent he'd set up a little ways away from the camp." Yawn.

See what I mean? All of a sudden the action slows down.

But, here's another rule for writers! Extra stuff (or exposition) *must be important* to the plot. It's got to play a good strong role.

The question is, therefore, how does this section, this extra stuff about what Moses did, fit into the plot of the golden calf story?

You might have guessed it already. This passage of exposition makes very clear that the Lord's promise to Moses has not been forgotten. You might remember how God said in verse 3 of this chapter that after the Israelites' betrayal, the Lord God would no longer dwell with them.

But that didn't mean God was planning to trek off to some other region of the Mesopotamian basin and find a whole new tribe of folks to love.

It did mean that God's home would no longer be found right in the heart of the camp. This passage indicates that God was still "with" the Israelites. This time, though, God's tent was pitched outside the camp, just as God had said.

God finds it hard to let people go. That's explanation, of course—extra stuff. But it's also the plot of our lives. In fact, the way God sticks around those people is more than just a story—it's the whole truth.

God loves us. And that's what makes the whole story so rich.

··

Sometimes we feel so far away, Lord, as if you have wandered to the outskirts of our lives. Actually it is we who have left you. Thank you for holding onto us so firmly. Amen.

TEACH ME THY WAY

....

Read Exodus 33:12-13

I'll grant you this: if any human being had good reason to trust God, Moses did. If we were to count the miracles Moses witnessed since he first heard God's voice at the burning bush, the list would run as long as this page. Moses, more than any of us, should have been sure of God's hand.

Wrong.

Moses, like the rest of us, was human. And the story in today's passage indicates that every last human heart pumps fear as well as blood. Who really trusts God?

Let's take Moses, make him female, then put him in Hollywood. Here goes:

Christianne tried out for *The Sound of Music* when she was eight. Her sister's high school needed some elementary school kids for the youngest Trapp family members, and she was chosen.

Four nights in a row the theater was packed with people. Then all those weeks of rehearsal—almost three months—were worth it, she thought. Twice she got a standing ovation, and it thrilled her to the core.

Playing in *The Sound of Music* had given Christianne the bug. She quit summer softball because she wanted, like nothing else, to be on stage. Twice more before high school she played roles in community theater productions.

In high school she spent most of her time, outside of studying, in plays and music. She took voice lessons and modern dance, and whenever the school put on a show, you could count on Christianne being somewhere up front, shoulders back, head held high, the focus of most everyone's attention.

She went to college on a theater scholarship—theater and music. She starred in a number of college productions, did summer stock theater for three years, and after graduation, entertained at Disney World.

All through those years, Christianne felt deeply that what the Lord wanted with her life was performance. She really believed that she'd been given marvelous gifts in music and theater, and she was absolutely convinced that the Lord wanted her to use her talent.

Christianne is now twenty-three. She lives in a shoddy part of Los Angeles. Although she's made a few commercials and had a couple of add-on roles in movies, she makes her living scooping dips at a Baskin Robbins. There are times, on hot days when the store is full of little picky kids, when she wonders if she's right about what the Lord wants from her.

She prays a lot. "All through my life," she says to God, "you've given me the sense that you wanted me to be in music or theater—for all these years," she says. "Can't you give me a sense of what's ahead here? I get discouraged. I get down. I want to know whether I should be here. I want to know whether I should just quit, or if I should keep on going. Please, Lord," she says, "tell me what's ahead."

Now, back to the desert. What Moses really wants from God—even though he's already had such vivid indications that God is with him and his people—is some additional commitment. "Teach me your ways, Lord," he says.

More than anything, Moses needs deep assurance that all of the struggle and the heartache is really going to go somewhere—that the whole business is worth it.

"Teach me your ways," he says. "I want to know."

Don't we all?

....

*Lord, come into our lives the way you were in
Moses' life. Show us your hand. Help us to
understand your world, and use us as your people.
In Jesus' name, Amen.*

SHOW ME!

....

Read Exodus 33:17-23

God's first set of stone tablets have already seeped into the Israelite ecosystem. Not content merely to smash them into smithereens, Moses has the people drink of his specially brewed unholy water.

Now, if anything is clear about this whole sad story, it's this: the I AM demands our respect. Whatever God tells us, God takes seriously, even when we don't. The Lord will not tolerate our disrespect. Three thousand Israelites have already paid for their disrespect with their lives.

But today's passage, like some Psalms, presents a picture of a human being—in this case, Moses, of course—who sounds almost disrespectful. David can sound that way too at times. Moses certainly doesn't mock or insult God, or talk behind God's back. That's not the kind of disrespect I mean.

This is another, maybe less ugly, kind of disrespect. All of us use it at one time or another, usually toward people in authority over us. Imagine this: I walk into my boss's office, take a look at him, then say, "That's a new suit, isn't it? Stand up. Let me see it."

We may well live in a society where nothing is sacred, but unless I know my boss really, really well, making any kind of demand on him isn't particularly smart, not even if it's only asking to see his new suit.

The way Moses makes demands of God in today's passage is really interesting. After pleading with God not to abandon the Israelites (vv. 15-16), after hearing God's pledge not to abandon them (v. 17), now Moses stands before the Lord God Almighty. And almost out of the blue, Moses puts his hands on his hips and says, "All right, as long as you're in a good mood, show me your glory. Go on, show me."

He doesn't come to God whimpering, down on his knees. He doesn't seem to tremble or shake. He's not bawling. He's just standing there, and this harebrained idea jumps into his head: I want to see the God behind this voice I hear. "All right, show me," he says.

Now, God could well have said something like this: "Who are you, you clod, to think you can demand anything of me? I am the I AM, and nobody even moves on this chessboard you call earth without my say-so."

God could have snapped back at Moses' outrageous demand, but that doesn't happen. Instead, God gives an odd little show. "I'm going to hide you in a little slit on a mountain," says the Lord. "I'm going to pass by you, but I'm going to hold my hand in front of your face. I'll let you see this much, Moses—my backside. When I'm past you, I'll give you just a peek—that's it."

Moses makes this outrageous demand, and God cooperates—to an extent. God lets him see what all of us can see: just a fraction of the reality of God's goodness, grace, and love. None of us have seen God, not even Moses. No one really fully and completely *knows* God.

What happens in this little passage—Moses "seeing" God—is called a *theophany* by Bible scholars. And what's most remarkable about this theophany is what it says about the relationship between Moses, God's main man, and God Almighty. They're really close.

You see, only people who know each other really, really well can make those kinds of demands and get away with it. I could tell my boss to stand up and show me his new suit, but only *if I know him well.*

Moses, like David, knows God well. So can we. Moses can really talk to God. So could David. And so can we. It's not disrespect at all.

It's honesty, it's openness, it's even love.

....

Lord, help us to be honest with you. Help us to come to you with everything—not just our troubles and frustrations, but also our joys. Teach us how to talk to you often and always. Amen.

HANDEL'S MASTERPIECE

....

Read Exodus 34:1-9

George Frideric Handel wrote ten oratorios before sitting down to write his *Messiah*, and he composed another eleven after this most famous work was completed. It's tough to imagine Handel writing more after he'd completed his masterpiece. After *Messiah*, what could anyone do for an encore?

Writing—whether it's music or literature—is a lonely job. Committees don't write music. Handel must have spent hours at his desk and over a piano creating line after line, hoping that something he dreamed up would bring people joy.

Actually, Handel was somewhat depressed when he wrote the *Messiah*. He wasn't at the top of anybody's pop charts. In fact, not much of anything he'd written so far had caught on, and so he felt defeated and disillusioned. He must have wondered if he really should have been a roofer instead of a composer. If at first you don't succeed, it's not hard to have second thoughts.

The words for his *Messiah* were selected and arranged by a man named Charles Jennens. Handel took that libretto and began to write the music on August 22, 1741. He finished what he called "Part the first" just six days later, August 28, and then started immediately on the second part, finishing that music nine days later. "Part the third" took an additional six days, so that he was finished on Saturday, September 12.

I don't know if you have any sense for how long it usually takes to create music, and I'm not sure I do. But I'll say this much: writing the *Messiah* in the space of three weeks has to rank as one of the most incredibly intense outbursts of creative energy ever recorded.

Think of Michael Jackson, add Hammer, throw in the Beach Boys, Frank Sinatra, Judy Garland, and Diana Ross. Season with the Rolling Stones, Ice T, and Amy Grant. If the mixture still seems weak, bolster the whole mess with Elvis and the Beatles. Add any of your favorites— but chances are, none of their work will achieve the worldwide popularity of Handel's *Messiah*.

The story is told—and it may be myth—that once Handel put down the pen after those three weeks of writing, he said, "I have seen God."

Millions of people who listen to that music, whether it's performed by professionals in the world's great listening halls or by some community choir in a cattle barn, might well say the same thing. Everyone stands up, after all, for the Hallelujah Chorus.

But as great as Handel's masterpiece is, as reverent in tone, as comprehensive about redemption, as close as it brings us to the eternal mystery of God's own being, no one, not even Handel, has really seen God.

In today's passage, Moses is told that God's name, at least, will be revealed to him. Then God proceeds to deliver a whole paragraph of self-definition: "The Lord, the Lord, the compassionate and gracious God, slow to anger, abounding in love and faithfulness, maintaining love to thousands, and forgiving wickedness, rebellion and sin. Yet he does not leave the guilty unpunished; he punishes the children and their children for the sin of the fathers to the third and fourth generation."

"This is what you may see, Moses," God might have said. "This is what you must know. This is how I am defined."

And what God tells Moses is meant for us as well. "You want to know me? Here is what the I AM is. Believe, and you too will see God."

We all would like a vision of you, Lord. Like Handel, we'd love to claim that just once in our lives we really were able to see you clearly. Thank you for your Word—and thank you for your wondrous creation—for in both we see glimpses of who you are and how you love us. Amen.

THIS IS THE (GOOD) NEWS

....

Read Exodus 34:10-16

I know lots of people who have been Christians their whole lives, but who wish, just the same, they'd been saved only yesterday.

I grew up in a town that was full of believers, and now I teach in a Christian college. My father's family—as well as my mother's—were all Christians. In fact, they have been for generations. Throughout my whole life I've been surrounded by people who've been Christians almost since they were old enough to think.

But, like I said, I know lots of Christians who wish they'd just been saved.

Here's why. "If you've ever known any new Christians," these people say, "you know they're just plumb full of joy. Know what I mean?" [Sure I do.] "It's like lights have been turned on for the first time in their lives, and they just can't get enough of the Lord."

Nearly all of the great conversion stories are incredibly dramatic. How about Martin Luther flinging his inkwell at the devil and stumbling across the idea of justification by faith? How about John Newton, the big bad slave-dealing unbeliever, whose guts shook so badly in an ocean storm that he found God and wrote "Amazing Grace"? Or how about Paul, struck blind by a divine light while on his way to corral Christians in Damascus?

Who *wouldn't* want a dramatic conversion? It's boring to be what you are when you've really never known anything different.

Let's face it—converted Christians make headlines because they're news. "Saul Converts to Christianity"—that's a story. "Moses Speaks to Burning Bush"—that's headline stuff. "Jonah Saved by Whale"—wow!

"Jim Schaap Raised by Believing Parents." Yawn.

Maybe you've heard the old rule about news: "Dog Bites Man" isn't news. "Man Bites Dog"—that's news!

The great thing (I can only imagine this, of course) about being a new Christian is hearing the story of the gospel for the first time through believer's ears. Imagine how someone like Rahab, the converted prostitute, must have loved reading God's Word for the first time.

I bring this up because I realize, these days especially, just how hard it is to get fired up about God's promise to Moses in today's passage. It's the same old thing. If I've heard this once, I've heard it a thousand times: "I am making a covenant with you. Before all your people I will do wonders never before done in any nation in all the world." (As if the Lord hasn't already—how about those frogs?) "The people you live among will see how awesome is the work that I, the Lord, will do for you." (You think the Egyptians will ever forget the Passover?)

More of the same. Nothing new here. Nothing at all. At the very same time God is spelling out exactly how they are to live, the Israelites are caught in an act of disobedience—creating a dumb golden calf to take God's place. God gets really angry; blows Moses down the mountain; punishes thousands; then starts right in on the same old song: "I will make a covenant. . . ."

That's not news.

But it is the gospel. Whether you've read it for the first time just now, or whether you've known it your whole life long—the good news is this: God forgives because God loves. We are spared because the Lord cares.

That's what the whole story is about. And because we so often fail— new Christians and old ones—God's promise to all of us is really news, always and forever.

The good news of salvation, Lord, is that you love us.
Keep it ever fresh within us so that we never take
your love for granted. Thank you for
your forgiveness, over and over again.
In Christ's name, Amen.

MOSES AND THE GREAT TAN

....

Read Exodus 34:29-35

I'm going to shut down operations here. There's a lot more to the book of Exodus—six whole chapters, in fact. But most of what follows Moses' second return from the mountain are tabernacle specs and ceremonial laws, nearly word-for-word the same as those we've been over before Moses smashed the first stone tablets.

Besides, this is a wonderful place to quit—Moses with a great tan. Notice that Moses wasn't even aware of his radiant face himself. Imagine his reaction when the people of Israel shrank in fear as he came down the mountain. "Hold on," he probably said. "I'm not going to hurl these"—Moses points at the new stone tablets—"like I did the last set."

Some yokel probably said, "Moses, your—your—your face. . . ."

And maybe then Moses drew his sword and checked his reflection in the blade. That's when he knew he wasn't the same. Although the Bible says nothing about how he reacted to this new shine, my guess is he smiled.

Why? Maybe two reasons. First, he knew that he'd been granted what he wanted—a vision, no matter how fragmentary, of God. He'd seen something of God's radiance, even if it was only God's backside. This great tan he wore was caused by nothing less than a vision of God.

But he may have smiled for another reason too. You see, when they demanded an idol God's people really wanted a god they could *see*—not just a voice or a peal of thunder or even a spiralling cloud. They wanted something to feast their eyes on.

The I AM doesn't give the Israelites everything they want when Moses comes back down from the mountain, but they do get a present for the eyes. The minute they see Moses they know that not even six weeks of desert sun can lay down a tan the quality of his. They know Moses has been somewhere really special. They can *see* it.

Moses' great tan *shows* the people of Israel once more that the God of Abraham and Isaac, the God who had delivered them up miraculously from slavery in Egypt, the God who spread manna over the desert ground every morning, was their God. And their God was real.

It's absolutely amazing the way the Lord keeps on coming back.

The Bible says that Moses continued to veil his face, except in those moments when he visited the Lord. Most of the time, that great tan was hidden behind some kind of veil.

Maybe the tan stayed. Maybe this glimpse of God that Moses wanted so badly was enough to make Moses' own face shine forever.

You know, I'd like the story to end here. I'd like to be able to say, "Well, folks, from this time forward, everyone lived happily ever after."

But it ain't that way.

Israel shrugged off the promises God laid so clearly in front of them. They chased other gods and were eventually overrun by just about every vagabond gang in the valley. Moses died on a mountain overlooking Canaan, holding his binoculars, a couple of miles from the promised land.

But the old, old story is still news. God Almighty keeps coming back. The Lord is always there for us. When the people turned their backs on God, that same God sent another messenger with a radiant face. But this time the radiance was not from having seen God, but from *being* God. Bing, bing, bing!

The story is, God loves us, more than we know. We're God's people, blessed with God's glory to make a difference in the world.

And that's the really great news from the Mesopotamian valley.

*Thank you for loving us, Lord. May all of our lives
ring with thanksgiving for the goodness and mercy
you extend to us, your people. Thank you for
sending your Son, who died that we may live.
In his name, Amen.*